The T

Th

of Jesus of Nazareth

The eternal word,
the One God, the Free Spirit,
speaks through Gabriele,
as through all the prophets of God—
Abraham, Job, Moses, Elijah, Isaiah,
Jesus of Nazareth,
the Christ of God

The Ten Commandments of GOD

through Moses,
interpreted with the words
of the present time through the prophetess
and emissary of God, Gabriele

The Sermon on the Mount

of Jesus of Nazareth,
explained, corrected and
deepened by Christ Himself—
and revealed through the prophetess
and emissary of God, Gabriele

Gabriele
Publishing House

www.Radio-Universal-Life.org
www.gabriele-publishing-house.com
www.radio-santec.com
http://www.alternativartv.eu
www.editorialgabriele.com

"The Ten Commandments of God through Moses, interpreted with the words of the present time through the prophetess and emissary of God, Gabriele"
&
"The Sermon on the Mount of Jesus of Nazareth, explained, corrected and deepened by Christ Himself—and revealed through the prophetess and emissary of God, Gabriele"

1st Edition June 2022

Max-Braun-Str. 2, 97828 Marktheidenfeld
www.gabriele-verlag.com
www.gabriele-publishing-house.com

Translated from the original German title:

„Die Zehn Gebote Gottes & Die Bergpredigt des Jesus von Nazareth"

The German edition is the work of reference for all questions regarding the meaning of the contents.

Order No. S182TBEN

Printed by: KlarDruck GmbH, Marktheidenfeld, Germany

ISBN 978-3-96446-264-0

Table of Contents

The Ten Commandments of GOD

through Moses,
interpreted with the words
of the present time
through the prophetess and
emissary of God, Gabriele

Table of Contents

The Ten Commandments of God, interpreted with the words of the present time

Foreword

The letter comes alive only when we begin to fulfill the commandments. Through this we gradually mature into the all-encompassing law of love and of life. Only those who fulfill the commandments with their heart and in the spirit of love will recognize the all-encompassing law and thus, find their way to the truth, which is within, in the soul of the human being.

Through Moses, God gave humankind the Ten Commandments.

The Spirit of God is freedom. The free, eternal, omnipresent Spirit, called God in the western world, is omnipresent Being, omnipresent life. It is the power of the universe, the stream in the mighty suns and planets. It is the life in the Earth, in every plant, in every animal, in every stone and not lastly, in every person and in every soul. The omnipresent Free Spirit, God, is thus the All-power in all of infinity.

From the Eternal to His human children, the commandments of God through Moses are truly a gift of love and a help for life, excerpts from the all-encompassing eternal law of infinity. Since in the Spirit of the eternal Being, of the eternal life, everything is contained in all things, in each commandment, we can thus find the other commandments.

We human beings are given the task to fulfill the commandments of the All-One in our life on Earth, that is, to live them—not to merely know about them or read about them. The commandments of God do not forbid, because the Free Spirit is freedom, which says that a person is free to accept God's pointers and to live accordingly or to leave them.

Because God does not intervene in a person's life, we ourselves are responsible for our life, for the content of our feeling, sensing, thinking, speaking and acting.

The commandments of God are inherent principles of the laws, excerpts from the eternal law of the Kingdom of God. They help those who strive to fulfill them and to attain higher ethics and morals, through which our whole person becomes refined in our way of thinking, speaking and acting. Those who walk the path of the commandments of God also ennoble their senses and develop a higher perspective on their life; they recognize that nature and the animals are likewise a part of the divine unity. The commandments of God that are lived bring about freedom and a gain in life.

The commandments of God are an offer from God, the Free Spirit, to us human beings, so that we live accordingly, and by gaining higher ethics and morals, we learn to understand the meaning of justice, unity and love for God and neighbor. Based on this step-by-step fulfillment, the person draws closer to the life, which is the universal, Free Spirit: God, the All-Spirit in all things.

During the course of the step-by-step fulfillment of the commandments of God, we not only look deeper, but also experience in ourselves that the free, omnipresent Spirit is also in us.

May it be repeated: The life is God, the Free Spirit, who, in all cultures worldwide, is one and the same. In all cultures worldwide, the Free Spirit is the unending diversity and fullness of the Being. Every commandment of God is a gateway to the fullness of life, because God, the Free Spirit, is the life. If, by way of correct thinking and doing, we immerse in the depths of life, in the root of the Being, then we discover that every commandment contains a multiplicity of the Being and is contained in the other commandments as a source of strength. With the words "Free Spirit," which we call God in the western world, is not meant the "god" presented by priests and pastors.

As a human being, Jesus of Nazareth was the Son of God and, as a being in God, He is the Co-Regent of the Kingdom of God, the Christ of God, who, as Jesus of Nazareth, brought redemption and the path back to the Father's house. As Jesus of Nazareth, He taught the people that the eternal Father and He are one, which says: one Spirit, one love, one truth, the eternal truth, the unending, eternal law that makes you free. The Spirit of the Christ of God is in the Father, and the Father is in the Spirit of the Christ of God—one Spirit, one life, one truth.

For approximately 47 years, the Free Spirit, the Spirit of the Christ of God, has been giving revelations through His prophetess, His speaking instrument, who is also the emissary from heaven, Gabriele. The Christ of God, the Free Spirit, is not bound to any external religion, because—just as Jesus of Nazareth taught, and as the Christ of God teaches today—every person is the temple of God and therefore, needs no church made of stone to find God, the eternal

All-Intelligence, the eternal Spirit, in order to worship Him.

Today, the Christ of God speaks into the New Era.

God, the Eternal, is not changeable. He is the same, yesterday, today and tomorrow. This also applies to the Ten Commandments of God through Moses. The Christ of God, who reveals Himself during the present time, spoke into the heart of His prophetess and emissary of God, Gabriele, who, in her own words, passed on what is of particular significance for the New Era, because the idolatrous gods have increased in diversity.

If we believe in the Ten Commandments of God and if we also believe in Jesus, the Christ, in His teachings—and above all, in the heavenly teaching, the Sermon on the Mount of Jesus—if we call ourselves Christian or original Christian or describe ourselves as followers of Jesus of Nazareth, then, at the same time, we very automatically obligate ourselves to fulfill what we say we are.

May one thing be made clear: The fulfillment of what the Eternal gave us in the Ten Commandments and Jesus of Nazareth in His teachings and in the Sermon on the Mount has nothing to do with institutional church statutes and ecclesiastical decrees.

The First Commandment of God

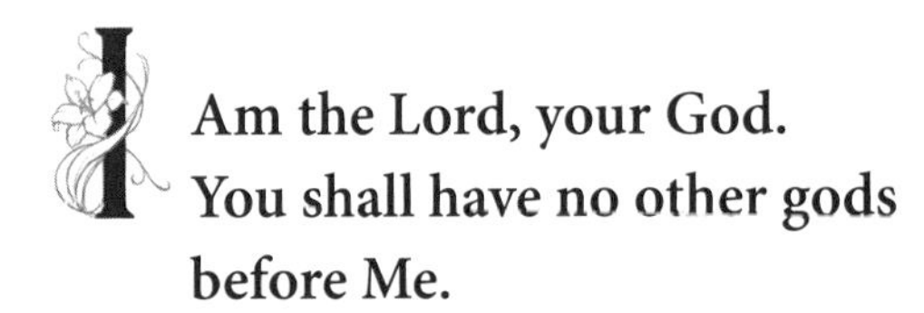

Am the Lord, your God.
You shall have no other gods before Me.

The God of Abraham, Isaac and Jacob, the God through Moses, through all the prophets of God, is the Free Spirit, the eternal law, the love for God and neighbor.

God, the Free Spirit, is the Creator-power in all things. Wherever we human beings go, wherever we look—in everything is the eternally prevailing Spirit. In every person, that is, in us, in our soul, is the Spirit of Truth, the Free Spirit. It touches us in every cell of our body and through our breathing. Everything that surrounds us, what we see and do not see bears the Spirit, God, who is the life.

In the very basis of their soul, human beings are divine, but they are not God. The divine being is eternally existent, because it was beheld and created by God, its heavenly Father. The pure being is also called spirit being.

The word of God, the commandment through Moses, teaches us: "*You shall have no other gods before me.*" What are the other gods, or idols, and how many additional idolatrous gods has humankind created for itself at the present time, to which many are addicted and which it worships? They are money, overdeveloped technology, craving for pleasure, addiction to gambling, claims to power, intense desires, cravings and passions and much more. All addictions have their corresponding idols, which these days are worshipped, so to speak, by many people worldwide. People worship people or honor those of whom they believe—or those who convey the belief to them—they were called by God to lead the people and to forcibly instruct them, in order to bind them. Many people pay tribute to gods, to idols, even to so-called high-ranking people, who let themselves be revered by the people.

The Kingdom of God is seven dimensional, as is the all-encompassing eternal law, God.

We human beings have received excerpts from the seven-dimensional, eternal law of God through Moses for our three-dimensional world: the Ten Commandments of God. The commandments of God that are lived could help us understand the all-encompassing life from God. Only with the step-by-step fulfillment of them, do we attain higher ethics and morals, and only on this path will our consciousness expand, which looks deeper and further.

Because the Kingdom of God is seven-dimensional, we should not make an image of the Kingdom of God, of heaven, nor of what is on, in and over the Earth. Let us take seriously the words of Jesus of Nazareth, who essentially taught us: *"The Spirit of God is in you, and you are the temple of the Holy Spirit."* Worshipped images, for example, statues and pictures of saints, imprint themselves in our soul as three-dimensional pictures. And when the hour comes in which the body, the shell of the soul, passes on, the soul goes into the realms of the beyond. Then, in and on it, adhere the three-dimensional images that do not resemble the seven-dimensional life. At some point, the soul will have to recognize that these inputs, the three-dimensional pictures that it worshipped as a human being, do not correspond to the seven-dimensional eternal life.

We people cannot imagine the Kingdom of God; neither can we make a picture of the purely spiritual worlds, nor of the spirit beings, whom we call angels, nor of God, our eternal Father, whom we also call the Father-Mother-God and worship in the Lord's Prayer, nor of Christ, the Co-Regent of the Kingdom of God, either. Pictures and statues merely correspond to our human world of imagination. For this reason, we should not worship images.

Nor should we worship the corpse of Jesus on the cross. His Spirit is risen and as the Son of God, as the Co-Regent of the Kingdom of God,

He sits at the right hand of the eternal Father. The Son of God, the Co-Regent of the Kingdom of God, is the Redeemer of all souls and human beings. He is the way, the truth and the life, and He, Christ, leads us to the eternal Father in the seven-dimensional eternal kingdom. The cross without a corpse, as the symbol of His Redeemer-deed, leads the way into the Kingdom of God, of peace, unity and freedom.

As we have read, the eternal Free Spirit is omnipresent life and thus, in every animal, in all plants, that is, in nature, in the minerals and in every stone. In each drop of water is the life. Everything in all things is the unity and the unity in God is the immortal life. We human beings, respectively, are merely the shell of the eternal life. Deep in the very basis of our soul, we belong to the Kingdom of God. Just as the physical body is merely the shell of the true life, so is each life form of earthly nature, every animal, every plant, every tree, every bush, every stone, merely the shell of the life. The life, the Creator-power, pulsates in everyone and everything; it is the Free Spirit, the eternal law of love for God and neighbor. In everything that we see and do not see, the all-encompassing, eternal life is active. Matter, the three-dimensional, is the shell; it is merely the reflection of God's creation, in which pulsates the seven-dimensional life.

The Second Commandment of God

You shall not take the name of God in vain.

How do we take the name of God in vain? For example, when we curse in His name, when we swear dishonorably or casually call out "Oh, my God!" without realizing that we are calling out the name of God without really having Him in mind. Or when we use words of greeting, such as "Greetings in God," commonly used in Bavaria, without realizing that we are uttering the absolute Intelligence.

In many a conversation, the term, "Oh, my God" or "Good Lord" is spoken. What are we thinking when we do this? Mostly they are merely empty words, clichés. However, as we know today, everything is energy. From this, it can be concluded that for every word that comes out of our mouth, we ourselves are responsible—not God. Every person who takes the name of God in vain abuses His name, thus wasting energy, through which they are punishing themselves. According to the law "action brings reaction," we ourselves are responsible for our thinking, speaking and acting—not the Almighty.

Christ calls upon us to question our thoughts and words, being aware of the following: What are we thinking and saying? Are our behavior patterns in accord with what we speak, for example, "Greetings in God," or "Oh Lord, oh Lord!"? Everything is energy. Thus, the question arises: Does God punish us when we offend against our own energy, since this also includes our life on Earth? No, we punish ourselves, when we decrease our life force, our energy.

Every now and then, we hear: "Thank God, I managed this or that, or this or that didn't happen!" Are we then truly thankful to God or is it merely spoken off-handedly, a turn of speech, a cliché? Unfortunately, it's only in the rarest cases that we take such situations seriously and as a reason to think about ourselves, about our behavior, our life, and not lastly, about the seed that we sow in the field of our soul with our thoughts and words, consciously or thoughtlessly and rashly done.

We should realize more and more often that our seed will sprout at some point or other. What then? It will become clear to anyone who believes in "action brings reaction," in sowing and reaping, in cause and effect, that the Eternal, whom we in the western world call God, does not punish. Consequently, He does not force us to do anything either, because, without exception, His commandments say "you shall" and not "you must." The commandments, in particular, are an offer, an orientation. People are free to think, to talk, to act however they want. Since we human beings are free, we are also responsible for our works, for everything that we feel, sense, think, say and do, day after day.

We should differentiate between "you must" and "we have to."

"You must" is personal; it is thought and spoken to the person and is thus against the freedom from God, which says, "you shall."

In contrast, the words "we have to" are impersonal, because they are spoken in a general sense and do not concern any person directly, unless it is an order. Then it turns personal and doesn't leave a person free. The result is a binding decision, which says: Divide, bind and rule!

God, the Eternal, merely offers the commandments through Moses from His heavenly law. In connection with the teachings of Jesus of Nazareth, above all, the Sermon on the Mount, they are the path into the Kingdom of God.

Christ is the Co-Regent of the Kingdom of God. His name, Christ, is also taken in vain, that is, abused, in many a political party. The name of the almighty God and that of His Son have nothing to do with politics. One wonders if He is, perhaps, supposed to merely be used as a figurehead, in order to blind people? Anyone who wants to check out the speeches of many people, including those in the so-called Christian political parties, and, in the end, their own personal behavior patterns, should read what Jesus recommended to us in the Sermon on the Mount as a distinguishing characteristic. Among other things, He taught us, *"You will know them by their fruits."*

Those who have a high regard for the Ten Commandments of God and the teachings of Jesus of Nazareth will recognize and comprehend the extent to which the name of the All-Highest and the name of Jesus, the Christ, are abused in so-called Christian political parties, communities, churches and the like. Each one of us must answer for what we pretend or adhere to before the law of infinity, before God and before ourselves. This is true even if we know of a wrong and remain silent and, moreover, feel that we belong to this association.

In the ecclesiastical institutions, there is talk of the punishing God. According to the law of free will, we punish ourselves when we know about the commandments of God and reject them. The law of infinity is the love for God and neighbor. It contains freedom. Those who follow church regulations, where it says "you must," who believe in eternal punishment, which is called damnation, have not yet thought about the abuse of the commandments of God and of the teachings of Jesus of Nazareth.

Over and over again, we are encouraged by the Eternal, the Free Spirit, to learn to understand the meaning of the words, also in regard to the commandments of God. Human words are merely shells, like human beings are merely the shell of the true life, the shell of their soul. Thus, human words are shells, comparable to a husk; it is the content that is decisive.

Only once we are willing to find the truth in the commandments of God and in the words of the Christ of God, by applying them in daily life, will we experience the Free Spirit, who neither coerces nor punishes.

How often do we hear or read about sowing and reaping, about cause and effect, about action brings reaction?

Like so much else, an old folk saying is often casually spoken, without looking deeper, for example: "*The one who will not listen must feel.*" Therefore, those who do not want to listen to the pointers given by the Eternal take their own path. They cannot blame others and certainly not the Free Spirit, called God in the western world, for the stumbling blocks that they put on their path themselves—certain contents of their feeling, thinking and speaking. When at some point or other, they fall over the hindrances that they put there themselves, their stumbling blocks, then in most cases, they blame God for them. The old folk saying is given just as little attention as the law, "*We will reap what we sow.*" Therefore, the one who will not listen must feel.

Those who have to feel their own inputs, their own stumbling blocks, should be aware that it is for having turned away from the commandments and the teachings of Jesus of Nazareth, from the ineffably many offers of a helping hand and aids from the Free Spirit, God. The worries and hardships, the suffering and much more are not the will of the Eternal, but the outflow of a person's irrational thinking and acting. When we have to feel our own fetters, then usually we don't attribute this to ourselves, but ask: "Why does God allow this?" Instead of this, we should rather ask: "Hey! Why do you allow this to happen to you?"

Above all, we should realize that the responsibility regarding the content of our feeling, thinking, speaking and acting lies solely with ourselves. Many a one could say, "But that has nothing to do with freedom. God should really help and support us; God should protect us!" The Eternal does indeed stand by us. He helps and protects us. But when we don't want this, when we reject His hand, by turning our backs on the commandments of God and the teachings of Jesus of Nazareth, then it will be similar to a family in which the father says to his daughter, his son, "Watch out! Don't do that, it has consequences." It can be that the daughter or son thinks: "Well, whatever father says—the present time is different, I'll do as I want." Despite the father's admonishing words, "Don't do that, it has consequences," it can be that the daughter or the son thinks: "What for, what kind of consequences?" Perhaps they defiantly say, even furiously: "We'll accept them." And what does the father perhaps say? "I can't tie you to my admonishing words. You have the freedom to do it, but each of you will have to bear the results from it."

It's similar with God, our heavenly Father: When someone does not want to, even though they know about the commandments of God through Moses and about the teachings of Jesus of Nazareth and think, "So what? I'm not interested in that; we're in a different era; I'll do whatever I want," then God will not force them to do anything. Nor will He punish them; for the person is free, because God, the Eternal, gave freedom to all beings and human beings as an innate good.

The eternal Spirit, God, and His Son, Jesus, the Christ, reconcile, forgive and support us, when we want this, when we go toward the one free, omnipresent Spirit and heed what He offered us: the excerpts from the eternal law of love for God and neighbor, the Ten Commandments, and from Jesus of Nazareth, the heavenly teachings, above all, the Sermon on the Mount.

Let us ask ourselves: From what should God, the Eternal, protect us—perhaps from what we have defiantly, that is, high-handedly, caused? Let us ask ourselves: If God were to do this, would we, from one day to the next, be more alert in terms of our own thinking and acting, letting go of the not good behavior that had led to the dissensions—or would we continue to do whatever we want?

The Third Commandment of God

emember the Sabbath day to keep it holy.

Today's employees have to adapt to the circumstances of their respective firms, so it cannot be said in principle that the seventh day must be the day of rest. In many cases, for example, for people who work in shifts or who work in gastronomy, it may be that the seventh day is not a day of rest.

No person is excluded from the eternal law, the law of love for God and neighbor, which includes freedom. No matter which free day we have, we should plan a few minutes of reflection, in order to think over the past days. What was good, what was less good or even bad? We can deduce something from everything or discern things from conversations, particularly when our level of feelings speaks up, in a positive as well as a negative sense. When we have a so-called uneasy feeling, it's helpful to apply the word "why," which we direct to our self.

The little word "why" can break down many things, which we may have forgotten or even repressed over the course of the past hours or days. We could also reflect on the fact that a mighty positive force is active in us, which we call God in the western world, and that wants to help and support us.

Should thoughts want to tell you to perhaps go to a chapel or church, in order to pray there, then read what Jesus of Nazareth taught us. For one thing, He taught us that every person is the temple of God and that God dwells in the soul of the person. For another, He taught us the following concerning prayer: *"But when you pray, go into your room and shut the door and pray to your Father who is in secret. And your Father who sees in secret will reward you."*

You, we, all people are free to pray, to think and act as each one of us wants. However, there is one thing we should not casually disregard: We ourselves are responsible for what we do or do not do, for our entire behavior.

The Fourth Commandment of God

You shall honor (respect) your father, and mother.

These days, people often honor themselves. And people honor people. For example, people are honored who contribute considerable research results to society or who are raised to higher social ranks by those positioned in government and state.

In our time, for instance, top athletes, actors and actresses and other artists, as well as people who display their luxury and wealth, are admired and honored. Children should also honor their father and mother. Thus, we should honor people.

We human beings are all equal before the face of God, brothers and sisters, children of one Father, who is in heaven, just as Jesus of

Nazareth taught us, when He spoke, for example, to those who taught the people in the name of the Eternal:

"But you are not to be called rabbi, for you have one teacher, and you are all brothers. And call no man your father on earth, for you have one Father, who is in heaven. ...The greatest among you shall be your servant. Whoever exalts himself will be humbled, and whoever humbles himself will be exalted."

No matter what titles someone acquires or with what dignities they adorn themselves—before the face of God they are equal to their neighbor, without titles and dignities. This also applies to those people whose child, whose son or daughter we are on Earth. The word of God is the eternal law, it is the true life. Among other things, it says: *"Bear one another's burden,"* which means that the one helps the other.

To pretend you are honorable or to let yourself be honored by others is not foreseen in the All-eternal, universal law of equality, freedom and unity. The love for God and neighbor includes the respect for one's neighbor, and thus, that we should respect each other and give honor to God, the omnipresent Spirit, who is the life in everyone and everything, by also respecting His Creation, which includes people, animals, nature and the Mother Earth. Only those who respect life honor God. Whoever destroys life disdains God.

The Fifth Commandment of God

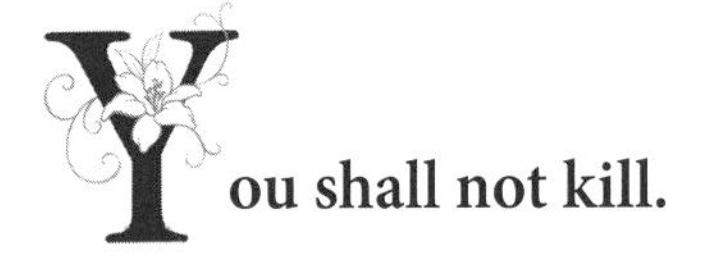

ou shall not kill.

The fifth commandment, in particular, is very broadly defined, because the institutional churches have changed the word "kill" into the word "murder." According to today's statement, we may kill in war, for example; on the other hand, premeditated killing is murder. If we take a close look at the word "war" in terms of what Jesus of Nazareth said, then we read what Jesus taught us, for instance, "... *all who take up the sword will perish by the sword.*"

Jesus of Nazareth was a pacifist, through and through. He taught peaceableness. Jesus of Nazareth was a man of peace and the Prince of Peace of heaven. Anyone who changed the word "kill" into "murder," thus weakening its meaning, is ultimately for war and against the teachings of Jesus of Nazareth. Before God, before the heavenly Father, of whom Jesus gave us an understanding, we are all brothers and sisters, who received the life, the eternal life, from God, our heavenly Father. We human beings breathe because the life, which is the almighty power, flows in our breathing. Who has the right, or who assumes the right, to take away the breath of their brother, their sister?

Jesus of Nazareth taught us that we do not have the right to kill a human being. This also applies to the deliberate killing of an animal or a plant filled with sap. We people are called upon to respect, love and cherish the Earth with all that is on it, in it and above it; for in all things is the life, and it is the all-prevailing Free Spirit, which alone is the life in everyone and everything.

Particularly present-day humankind is far from the eternal truth, which we call God in the western world. Unfortunately, very few think about the fact that He is the mighty Spirit of infinity, the Creator, whose life force prevails in all things. Whether it is the universes, the mighty suns and planets or the tiniest animal on Earth—everything bears the life from the eternal Spirit, the Creator of all Being. Therefore, who has the right to intervene in the life that is eternal? Who gave the life? Whose property is the life? The human being, the animal, all of nature has the right to live, and at that, until the earthly existence flows out. Thus, every person and all the nature kingdoms have the right to be as coarse-material existence until their time has come, in which they return as spiritual forms of life to the bosom of eternal life.

Present-day humankind mostly disregards the law of sowing and reaping—we will reap what we sow. When we look more deeply into our world of the arrogance and exploitation of people and nature, then we learn that the bad seed, the sowing, isn't ripening, but is already sprouting, that is, coming into effect. But who does this trouble? People think, the one more, the other less: "I am my own best friend. I am not meant." But you, all of us, are meant, because we bear the life and also bear our freedom, through which the law of the Fall developed, which says: Humankind will reap what it sows.

Thus, the one who consciously kills, whether it is in war or as a farmer or forester or hunter—no one has the right to deliberately kill. Whoever wantonly, that is, deliberately, kills is against the law of life and thus, against the Creator-God. The endpoint for each one is: What you sow you will reap at some point or other, for the soul of every person lives eternally. One day, the soul will go into the realms of the beyond and will have to bear what the person sowed.

The Sixth Commandment of God

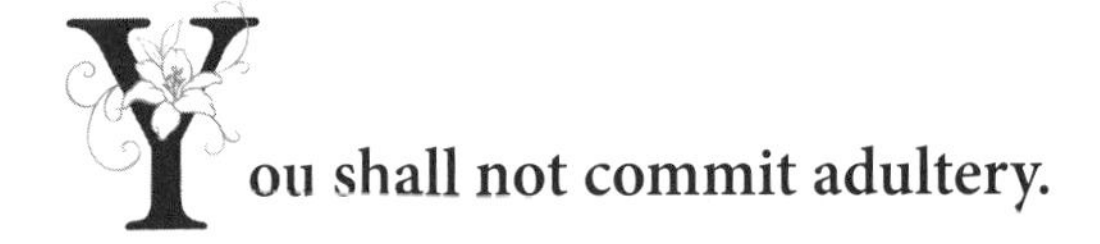

You shall not commit adultery.

Adultery is a breach of faithfulness, of trust. Marriages are usually made based on mutual trust. Whether the wife or the husband terminates the trust, by physically favoring another woman, or she another man, this person has broken the promise of mutual faithfulness.

Today's time appears to be not only fast-moving, but in relation to faithfulness, its pace is also taken into account with the idea that one has to enjoy life. The fast-moving pace of our time is also a force behind marriage and partnership, because today one promises to be faithful—tomorrow everything already looks very different.

It is similar in many businesses and enterprises. People sign a work contract, in which confidence in the firm is noted. But when one's own profit is involved, when perhaps beyond that, business machinations and manipulations play a role, then the work contract is often merely a piece of waste paper.

Wherever we look, today's time, today's world has become a sacrificial cult. In many cases, marriage and partnership are sacrificed for a short-lived affair. Whether there is a wife with or without a child, doesn't matter—the ostensibly fast-moving time demands its tribute. Whether it's adultery, as in breach of faithfulness, or breach of trust—it hardly matters anymore; one sacrifices their neighbor; one sacrifices a contractual signature. The forms of sacrificial cults are manifold. Life today can be compared to a game of dice. Today, the number one is the trustworthy one—tomorrow it may be number three, five or even number six, who is the confidant or the desired one.

And so, many a one thinks, "What do we still want with the commandments of God, which were given several thousand years ago to so-called Stone-Age people?" In all honesty: Don't many young people in this fast-moving time think this way or similarly, being of the opinion that today must bc lived—be it at the expense of others, or even at the cost of the grief and pain of those who were left behind and have to endure?

Even though we may consider ever so many abnormalities to be commonplace and are therefore not ashamed of them—God, the Eternal, is unchangeable. He is the same, yesterday, today and will also be so tomorrow. His eternal, cosmic law is absolute; it is the present. When in the sixth commandment of God it says, "*You shall not commit adultery,*" then this means, among other things: "You shall keep your promises," which means honorable faithfulness, or honorable trust, whether in marriage, in partnership, in big businesses, firms and the like. Just as the people of yesterday, of the so-called Stone Age, should measure their thinking and speaking, their entire behavior, on the commandments of

God, the same applies today in the so-called Age of Technology, which people call the Age of Enlightenment.

Marriage, partnership and contractual promises should also be sustained today with honesty, openness, faithfulness, straightforwardness and trust. Those who take seriously the commandments of God and for 2000 years, the teachings of Jesus of Nazareth, of the Christ of God, and fulfill them step by step, gain foresight and insight and can weigh, for example, whom they have before them as a person and to whom they can give their trust. Therefore, it says in the sixth commandment, "*You shall not commit adultery.*"

Breach is breach. What is repaired is no longer whole. Therefore, we examine ourselves first, before we commit an injustice, that is, let something be broken. This means that we should first think, before we break something, because fixing what is broken often costs much more time, and something fixed is simply fixed—it will never become whole. Many a thing that is broken up may perhaps find its just echo in the law of sowing and reaping, "*You will reap what you sow.*"

The Seventh Commandment of God

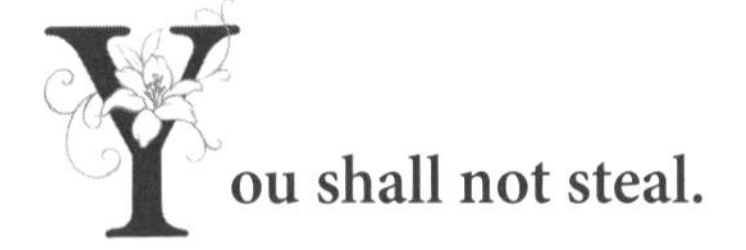

ou shall not steal.

The word "steal" could be divided into two categories. The first category is theft, the second category is stealing. How quickly we say, "But, but, I don't steal!" Can we claim this so easily when we know that everything is energy and that our time is also an energy factor?

Who is a thief? For example, we could call those people thieves who purloin money and valuable things. Others could be called thieves who steal the time of their fellow people, for example, who carry out long, useless conversations with lots of ifs and buts and don't get to the point; or they hold forth in so-called "small talk" and never get to the end; or when someone demands something from another, which they could have done themselves; or when the one quarrels with the other, because each one wants to be right and neither wants to concede to the other a little bit of factual accuracy.

Wasting time, which is like wasting energy, applies to many situations, in manifold variations, which cannot all be listed here. This and much more is the depletion of energy, whereby the one steals more or less energy from another. Each of us could certainly contribute a whole gamut of examples regarding what theft or stealing consists of.

But what's concerned here is not more knowledge about which forms of stealing exist, but what concerns each of us personally is the question: Why do I violate, why do we violate, the commandment, "*You shall not steal*"?

The Eighth Commandment of God

You shall not bear false witness against your neighbor.

To bear false witness means to speak untruth about another, to claim something untrue about oneself before the court and to make false statements about others. To tell our fellow people what they want to hear, to flatter them, to confirm them in their behavior, but also to think about them differently than what we say, is also deceitfulness and violates the eighth commandment.

The claim that our opinion is the truth can also be put in this category. An opinion always means that we don't precisely know. Our opinion, which we see as truth, is usually a thinking process on our side, a pattern of thought, something we've thought up and that seems logical to us. We then declare this as our opinion. But since an opinion bears witness to not-knowing, it can be untrue. That can be considered as bearing false witness.

To bear false witness could also be untrue gossip, which we spread, in order to achieve a certain purpose with it. With gossip, you can incriminate others. This also violates the eighth commandment.

Therefore, we should not bear false witness against our fellow people, but should think more often about ourselves, whether we have ourselves under control in terms of our thoughts and words, because what we emit is energy and comes back to us at some point or other—whether we spoke or speak out the truth or untruth. Before conversations, those who demand moral values should ask themselves the question: Is what I want to say truthful? Or would it be a false witness against my neighbor?

When we make the effort to think about the eighth commandment, about bearing false witness, and that everything is energy, including our thoughts, then we should realize that we, every single one of us, are the guarantors for what we emit—whether it is the energy of thoughts, words or deeds. Can we guarantee that what we say corresponds to the truth? For this reason, we should be the monitoring mechanism over ourselves, the scales.

We should become more and more clear about the fact that everything is energy and that every bit of energy that we emit—whether positive or negative—comes back to us. To deliberately bear false witness can be called lying.

The Ninth Commandment of God

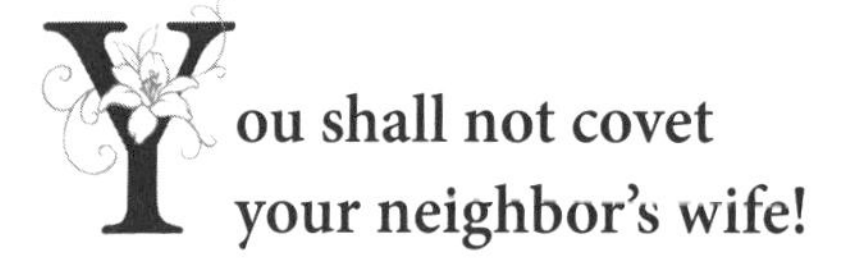

ou shall not covet your neighbor's wife!

The word "covet" contains desire, wanting to possess, the desire to take what I covet and consider it my property. The "mine" and "for me," wanting to make something my own can be broken down into the one word "covet." When we want to make our coveting come true, then in the meaning of the ninth commandment, the wife, that is, the woman, is the property of the one who has acquired her through desire. Figuratively speaking, we can then say that she, the woman, has become the slave of the one who willfully and knowingly coveted her.

The same can be applied to the man, the husband, or even to a child, who is coveted, that is, abused, for physical purposes. When a man covets a woman or a woman a man or even a man a child, then the question automatically arises: for what purpose? As stated, desire is usually related to the body, through which dependency often develops, that is, modern slavery. If the female slave or the male slave—culminating in compulsive child abuse—has been enjoyed to the full and thus, is no longer of interest, then bitterness, emptiness, a feeling of being thrown away and exploited becomes widespread in those who have been dropped. The child that was robbed of its innocence is left behind, often empty, physically and mentally burnt out. From this, hatred and perhaps even the desire for revenge often develop.

And it would be better for someone who covets and abuses a child if they had not been born. Jesus said the following drastic words about this: "*... But whoever causes one of these little ones who believe in me to sin, it would be better for them to have a great millstone fastened around their neck and to be drowned in the depth of the sea.*"

The word "covet" has other aspects, such as furtively luring away so-called skilled personnel from big businesses and firms, in order to bring in their "know-how" or to spy out company secrets, whereby both concern prestige and money. Figuratively speaking, this can also be called a slave trade. Many more, even countless, examples could be given. But may one thing be established: Desire has very different facets.

In any case, let it be said that those who can be purchased and fall for the coveting, the desire, become modern slaves, who hand themselves over to their purchaser and thus, are and remain un-free, until they remember what would actually be the first step toward freedom. It is:

Stay true to yourself!

The second step could be: Pay attention to the lines that are laid out to catch you. The third step would be: Don't let yourself be lured away—make your own application, by acquiring a good, specialized professional training, which gives you joy and with which you earn your salary; for all good workers are worthy of their salary. The fourth step could be: Watch out for flattery, which comes before coveting and desire. Ask yourself: What happens when the train of lust has left the station—who are you then? Perhaps a burnt-out car that doesn't really know which sidetrack it's standing on ...

The Tenth Commandment of God

You shall not covet anything that belongs to your neighbor.

The tenth commandment of God through Moses lets us look deeper, when we look at our Earth, which God gave to all people, so that it could nourish His human children.

What has humankind made of the planet Earth? Ultimately, an island of parcels. Those who have inherited or acquired money and property possess a correspondingly large piece of land, a large parcel of land, which they call their property. Others possess only a little piece of this big, divided-up cake of parcels called Earth. Still others have no parcel of their own; they are workers who earn their bread and that of their family. They, their wives and children live from these earnings, just scraping by.

The owners of large parcels, the big capitalists, have the work done by so-called workers and employees on the parcel they own, their parcel island. They themselves live splendidly and enjoy—ultimately, through the work of others—the "mine" and "for me" that is their life. They don't need to earn their daily bread like the workers, the employees, do; the others do it for them. The workers, the employees, receive their salary from this and the owners their capital, which they invest accordingly, in order to thus increase their "property."

This inequality, which is growing ever greater, can lead to envy, hatred, covetousness and the like and cannot be denied, when we think about the fact that in our time, the rich are becoming ever richer and the poor ever poorer.

And how much more clearly does the tenth commandment ring in our ears today. Already Jesus of Nazareth said, *"It is easier for a camel to go through the eye of a needle than for a rich person to enter the Kingdom of God."* This statement can be related to the parceling of the planet Earth. The words of Jesus trouble the rich even less than formerly, since even more heart was weighed on a personal test stand, and the works of neighborly love were measured. Today, everyone is their own best friend.

But what counted yesterday also counts today. No one can take their money and property along with them into the beyond. Just as it was for the rich earlier, so is it also today. No one can go through the so-called eye of a needle, because the heavenly kingdom is still far away for the wealthy. Where then, will their poor soul be when their wealth no longer counts? The law of sowing and reaping will bring it all into balance. For this reason, it is not worth it to covet your neighbor's property. In any case, the Earth is God's planet and not the work of human egoism!

Those who comprehend the meaning of the Ten Commandments of God through Moses recognize that without the word of God that is lived, people do not know who they are and why they are living in the temporal as a human being.

The Sermon on the Mount

of Jesus of Nazareth,
explained, corrected and
deepened by Christ Himself—
and revealed through the prophetess
and emissary of God,
Gabriele

Table of Contents

Introduction

Nearly two thousand years ago, Jesus of Nazareth gave humankind the Sermon on the Mount. We can take essential parts of this teaching from the Bible. (Mat. 5-7) The Sermon on the Mount contains the essence of Jesus' teachings—core statements for a life according to God's laws, pointers for dealing with our fellow human beings, with animals, with nature. Those who put these teachings into practice in their daily life will very soon feel that their life changes, that it becomes peaceful and positive.

On the other hand, church leaders and politicians of the so-called Christian world claim that this teaching is a utopia and cannot be put into practice.

Was Jesus of Nazareth thus a utopian?

Or was He the realist, who could show us human beings the path out of the maze of the human ego?

Christ, the Son of God, passed over this Earth as Jesus of Nazareth. Since the "It is finished" on Golgotha, His Spirit of Redemption lives and works in each and every one of us. Over the past two thousand years, He has spoken again and again through the mouth of prophets. Today, in this mighty time of upheaval, He reveals Himself again through His prophetess. He explains and deepens His teachings, which He gave to the people as Jesus of Nazareth. This is done in His great work of revelation "This Is My Word. A and Ω. The Gospel of Jesus. The Christ-Revelation which True Christians the World Over Have Come to Know."

The book at hand contains an excerpt from this epoch-making work, which goes way beyond the content of the Bible. It gives a powerful overview of what was, of what is and of what will be. In this revelation, Christ gives humankind all-encompassing indications for a truly spiritual life according to the divine laws. Thus, in this work, His words are fulfilled, which He gave as Jesus of Nazareth, *"I have much more to say to you ..."* (John 16:12) Building on the "Gospel of Jesus," an existing, apocryphal gospel text, Christ describes in this book, "This Is My Word," His life and work as Jesus of Nazareth. He especially shows us *how* we can live in our time according to the laws of God, according to the Ten Commandments and the Sermon on the Mount, and He gives us a preview into the future, into His Kingdom of Peace on the Earth.

Jesus' Sermon on the Mount contains the essence of the Inner Path, which Christ teaches today through His prophetic word in all its steps and details. The Inner Path is the path of self-recognition and of overcoming human faults out of love for God.

The one who successfully follows this path to selflessness, equality, freedom, unity, brotherhood and justice, receives the strength to fulfill the Sermon on the Mount and the Ten Commandments more and more in daily life—also in occupation and business.

The book at hand wants to make the Sermon on the Mount of Jesus more accessible to all searching people—not only the parts recorded in the Bible, but the teachings with explanations and deepenings, which Christ has given to humankind today through His prophetic word. Beyond that, this book should give the reader insight into the depths of the work of revelation, "This Is My Word. A and Ω. The Gospel of Jesus. The Christ-Revelation, which True Christians the World Over Have Come to Know."

In this work, Christ builds on the book, "The Gospel of Jesus. What was 2000 years ago?" However, because some things in it are incomplete and sometimes have been handed down incorrectly, Christ explains and corrects this text today. Those passages that the Lord does not go into detail about essentially agree with the truth of His life and work as Jesus of Nazareth. Beyond that, Christ deepens and expands on important reports in "The Gospel of Jesus." Thus, in the complete work of "This Is My Word" humankind now has been given the complete truth, all significant aspects of the life of Jesus and of His teaching.

In the book "This Is My Word," One or more verses of the "Gospel of Jesus" are each followed by the words with which Christ, in 1989, explains, corrects and deepens these passages. This structure is also maintained in the reproduction of the excerpts here at hand. Headings have been placed to subdivide the text and make it clear.

The present book also contains the Twelve Commandments of Jesus, which Christ now has again given to humankind in His work of revelation, "This Is My Word" (Chap. 46:7-21). They are essentially the Ten Commandments that God revealed through Moses, and which Jesus of Nazareth expanded for His coming Kingdom of Peace on Earth.

For those readers who would like to actualize the commandments of Jesus' Sermon on the Mount in their lives, the following information will also be of importance: In 1991, after the full content of His Sermon on the Mount and after the revelation of the path to God in the innermost part of every human being, Christ still revealed to us the highest possible, the Absolute Law, in His work, "The Great Cosmic Teachings of Jesus of Nazareth to His Apostles and Disciples Who Could Understand Them. The life of the true God-filled people." It is the law of the heavens, given as a further help to all those who have set out to again become pure of heart through the fulfillment of God's laws.

God gave and gives. He does not ask whether people recognize His word, the divine word, and live accordingly. Each one can examine it and decide for themselves. May the one who can grasp it, grasp it.

Gabriele Publishing House—the Word

The Beatitudes

When Jesus saw the multitudes, He went on a mountain. And when He had sat down, the twelve came to Him. He looked up at His disciples, saying:

Blessed in the spirit are the poor, for theirs is the Kingdom of Heaven. Blessed are those who grieve, for they shall be comforted. Blessed are the meek, for they will possess the Earth. Blessed are those who hunger and thirst for righteousness, for they shall be satisfied.

Blessed are the merciful, for they will attain mercy. Blessed are the pure in heart, for they will behold God. Blessed are the peacemakers, for they will be called children of God. Blessed are those who are persecuted for righteousness' sake, for theirs is the Kingdom of God.

Blessed are you, when men will hate you and exclude you from their company and speak all sorts of evil against you and outlaw your names, for the sake of the Son of Man. Rejoice in that day and leap with joy, for behold, your reward is great in heaven. For their forefathers did the same to the prophets. (Chap. 25:1-4)

Christ explains, corrects
and deepens the word:

The Sermon on the Mount is the Inner Path to the heart of God, which leads to perfection.

The blessed ones will behold the Christ and, in all meekness and humility, will possess the Earth with Me, the Christ. Happy those who behold the glory of the Father-Mother-God in all things! They have become living examples for many.

I guide My own to the recognition of the truth.

Those who are of the truth hear My voice, because they are the truth and thus hear and perceive the truth as well.

The blessed ones are fearless and joyful; for they perceive and hear what those do not see and hear, who still hide behind their human ego, holding on to it with utmost effort so that they are not recognized.

However, the blessed ones look into the prison of the human ego and recognize the most deeply hidden thoughts of their fellow people. With the power of their light-filled consciousness, they shine into it and call out to their fellow people:

"Blessed in the spirit are the poor, for theirs is the Kingdom of Heaven!"

The words "the poor" do not mean material poverty. It is not this that brings bliss in the spirit, but the devotion to God, out of which the person fulfills what is the will of God. This is inner wealth.

The words "the poor" mean all those who do not strive for personal possessions and do not hoard goods. Their thinking and striving aim at the community life, in which they administer the goods that God has given to everyone in a lawful way. They do not put all their thoughts and energies on having worldly things. They serve the common good and extend their arms to God and consciously walk the path to the inner life. Their goal is the Kingdom of God in their inner being, which they want to proclaim and bring to all people who are of good will. Their inner wealth is the life in God, for God and for their neighbor. They live the commandment "pray and work."

They strive toward the Spirit of God and receive from God what they need for their earthly life and even more. These are the blessed in the Spirit of God.

"Blessed are those who grieve, for they shall be comforted."

The grief of human beings does not come from God, but it is either the grieving ones who have caused it themselves—or their souls have taken over a part of the debt of a brother or sister soul in the realm of the souls, to pay off that debt in the earthly existence, so that the brother or sister soul can enter higher spheres of inner life.

God's mercy is granted to those who bear their grief without accusing their neighbor and who recognize their faults and weaknesses in the grief, repent of them, ask for forgiveness and forgive. God, the Eternal, wants to comfort His children and take away from them what is not good and beneficial for their soul; for when the grief leaves the soul, that is, when the causes which became effective in the soul are settled, these people find their way closer to God.

"Bear your grief" means: Do not complain about it; do not accuse God or your neighbor. In your grief, find your sinful behavior that led to this grief.

Repent, forgive and ask for forgiveness, and no longer do what you have recognized as sin. Then the debt of the soul can be erased by God and thereupon you receive increased strength, love and wisdom from Him.

If you meet grieving and sorely afflicted persons and they ask you for help, then support and help them as far as it is possible for you and as it is good for their soul. And when you see that your neighbors thankfully accept the help and build themselves up with it, then give them even more, if it is possible for you.

However, you who give help, do it selflessly. If you do it merely as an outer obligation, you will receive no spiritual reward—and you will render no service to the soul of the person who is suffering and is sorely afflicted, but only to his body, to the vehicle of the soul.

"Blessed are the meek, for they will possess the Earth."

Meekness, humility, love and kindness go hand in hand. The ones who have become selfless love are also meek, humble and kind. They are filled with wisdom and strength.

People in My Spirit, the selflessly loving ones, will possess the Earth. Oh see, the path to the heart of God is the path into the heart of selfless love. The peace of God flows out of selfless love.

The people who journey toward the heart of God and the people who already live in God work for the New Era, by teaching all willing people the path to God. In this way, they take more and more possession of the Earth in My Spirit.

"Blessed are those who hunger and thirst for righteousness, for they shall be satisfied."

Those who hunger and thirst for the righteousness of God are seekers of truth, who long for the life in and with God. They shall be satisfied.

My brother, My sister, you, who long for righteousness, for the life in and with God, take heart and raise yourself out of the sinful human ego! Rejoice, for the time has come in which the Kingdom of God draws closer to those people who endeavor to keep the commandments of life.

Behold, I, your Redeemer, Am the truth in you. And so, in you, I Am the way, the truth and the life.

The truth is the law of love and of life. In the Ten Commandments, which are excerpts from the all-encompassing law of God, you find the mnemonic phrases for the path to the truth. Keep the Ten Commandments and you reach the path of the Sermon on the Mount more and more, on which the path to the truth is fundamentally carried out.

The path to the truth is the path to the heart of God, to the eternal life, which is selfless love. The Sermon on the Mount is the path into the Kingdom of God, into the laws for the Kingdom of Peace of Jesus Christ. If you delve deeper into them and fulfill them, you attain divine wisdom.

Recognize that no one should hunger or thirst for righteousness. Take the first step toward the kingdom of love by first being righteous to yourself. Practice a positive way of living and thinking and you will very gradually become a righteous person. Then you will bring the righteousness of God into this world; and you will also represent this, because you fulfill the will of God, of the Lord, out of His love and wisdom.

Recognize: The time is near when what was prophesied will take place. The lion will lie by the lamb, because the people have gained victory over themselves—through Me, their Redeemer. Thcy will form a great family in God and will live in unity with all animals and with all of nature.

Be glad, for the Kingdom of God has drawn close—and, with the Kingdom of God, I, too, your Redeemer and bringer of peace, the ruler of the Kingdom of Peace, of the World Kingdom of Jesus Christ.

"Blessed are the merciful, for they will obtain mercy."

The mercy of God corresponds to the meekness and kindness of God and is, for all souls, the gate to the perfection of life. The people who have unfolded in their souls all seven basic powers of life—the law, from Order to Mercy—through Me, the Christ, I, who live in the Father-Mother-God, will, as pure spirit beings, again enter the selfless love through the gate of mercy. They will enter the Kingdom of God, the heavens, and live in peace. The seventh basic power, the Mercy—called kindness and meekness in the Spirit of God—is the gate to the eternal Being. All people who practice being merciful will also attain mercy and will stand by those who are on the way to mercy.

Recognize that the path to the heart of God is the path of the individual in community with those of like mind, for God is unity, and unity in God is community in and with God and with one's neighbor.

The one who has taken the first steps on the path to perfection will fulfill the commandment of unity: One for all, Christ—and all for One, Christ.

As revealed, the Sermon on the Mount is the path of evolution toward the inner life. All those who are further ahead on this path of unfoldment toward the heart of God help, in turn, those who are just at the beginning of the path. In and over all, shines the Christ, who I Am.

"Blessed are the pure in heart, for they will behold God."

The pure heart is the pure soul which has again achieved the state of being an absolute spirit being through Mc, the Christ in the Father-Mother-God.

The pure souls that have again become beings of heaven are then the image of the eternal Father once more, and behold the Eternal face to face again. At the same time, they see, live and hear the law of the eternal Father, because they have again become spirit of His Spirit—the eternal law itself.

As long as people and souls still have to listen for the Spirit of God in themselves, they are not yet spirit of His Spirit, not yet the law of love and of life itself.

However, those who have again become the law of love and of life behold the eternal Father face to face and are in constant conscious communication with Him. They also perceive the law of God, the life from God, as a whole, because they are themselves the life and the love, and move in them. Whoever moves in the Absolute Law of God has also opened it up completely—from Order all the way to Mercy. All the seven basic powers of infinity serve them, because they are in absolute unity and harmony with all Being.

"Blessed are the peacemakers, for they will be called children of God."

According to their meaning, these words mean: Blessed are those who keep peace. They will also bring true peace to this Earth, because they have become peaceable within themselves. They are consciously the children of God.

"Blessed are those who suffer persecution for righteousness' sake, for theirs is the Kingdom of God."

Recognize that the one who followed Me was not respected by the worldlings, because I, too, as Jesus, was held in disdain by them. At all times, people who stepped into the true following of the Nazarene had to endure and suffer a great deal.

The Calls of Woe

Woe unto you who are rich! For you have received your consolation in this life. Woe unto you who are sated, for you will hunger. Woe unto you who laugh now, for you will mourn and weep. Woe unto you when all people speak well of you, for so did their forefathers with the false prophets. (Chap. 25:5)

Christ explains, corrects and
deepens the word:

"Woe unto you who are rich! For you have received your consolation in this life."

People who look upon their wealth as their property are poor in spirit. Many who are rich in earthly goods were given the spiritual task for their earthly life in the cradle, to be an example to those rich people who bind themselves to their wealth with hardened, unyielding hearts and whose sole thinking and striving is to increase this wealth for themselves. The people who are rich in earthly goods and have recognized that their wealth is a gift—which they have received from God only to bring it into the great whole for the well-being of everyone and to administer it there in the right way for all—are the ones who actualize the law of equality, freedom, unity and brotherhood. They contribute as a selfless giver so that the poor do not live in privation and the rich in luxury.

In this way, a balance is gradually established, an upper middle class for all those who are willing to selflessly fulfill the law "pray and work." Thus, very gradually, the true humanity of a community grows, whose members do not collect personal earthly riches, but rather consider everything to be common property given to them by God.

If rich people consider money and property as their own and are esteemed in the world because of their wealth, then, as the effect of their causes, they will live in poor countries in their next life on Earth and there beg for the bread that, as a rich person, they once denied the poor. This will happen as long as such incarnations are still possible.

The soul of such rich people will also find no rest in the spheres of purification. The souls that are poor in light and had to endure suffering and hunger in the earthly garment because of them will recognize them again as those who denied them what could have helped them out of the entanglement of the human ego. Many will accuse them, and then their soul itself will feel how the others suffered and hungered. In this way, a soul that was rich and esteemed as a human being in the earthly garment may suffer great hardship; this hardship is much greater than if it had had to beg for bread in the earthly garment.

Recognize that according to the laws of the Eternal, everyone who selflessly keeps the commandment "pray and work" is due the same; for God gives everyone what they need and beyond that. However, as long as this commandment is not yet observed by all people, there will be the so-called rich on Earth. It is their task to divide their accumulated wealth and to live just as those who selflessly fulfill the commandment "pray and work." If in this way, they think of the welfare of all and not of their own, the inner wealth will gradually turn without and no person will hunger or live in want.

Woe to you, you rich ones, you who call your money and property your own and make your neighbor work so that your wealth may increase! I say to you, that you will not behold the throne of God, but will continue to live where the feet of God are—on the Earth, again and again in earthly garments, as long as this is still possible. Even if you promote social service establishments, but you yourselves are so much wealthier than those who are supported thereby, then you are nevertheless servile to the satan of the senses, who wants the differences between rich and poor.

Through these differences, power and subservience, envy and hatred emerge. These give rise to dispute and wars. For this reason, those who cling to their wealth, even though they now and then think of the social good, serve the satan of the senses and act against the law of life: against equality, freedom, unity and brotherliness.

Those who consider money and property as their own and hoard them for themselves, instead of letting these material energies flow, are, according to the law of life, thieves, for they deprive their neighbor of a part of their spiritual heritage, for everything is energy. The one who ties it up through "mine" and "for me" acts against the law, which is flowing energy.

"Woe unto you who are sated, for you will hunger."

The wealthy, sated people who fill only "their" barns are empty at heart. They know only the mine and thine. Their senses and thoughts revolve around "my" property, "my" possessions, "my" bread, "my" food. "All this belongs to me"—this is their world. Such people will one day hunger and live in want until they realize that everything is the Being. Everything belongs to God and to all people who strive to do the works of God: To fulfill selfless love and the law of life for the Earth, "pray and work."

Those who speak only of mine and thine are light-poor people who already in this incarnation are preparing another sojourn on Earth or a long pilgrimage of their soul in the realm of the souls and, in both cases, in the garment of a beggar.

The soul that is dazzled by material things unconsciously hungers for light, because it is poor in light. It compulsively tries to compensate for this with outer things, such as earthly wealth, greed, gluttony, alcoholism or other cravings and pleasures. It is insatiable.

"Woe unto you who laugh now, for you will mourn and weep."

Those who laugh and mock their neighbor will one day be very sad and will cry over themselves—because they misjudged those whom they made fun of and mocked. they will have to recognize that, in the end, they have laughed at, scorned and ridiculed themselves; for the ones who judge and condemn their neighbors, who laugh at them, who scorn and ridicule them, judge, condemn, laugh at, scorn and ridicule Me, the Christ.

Recognize: Those who sin against the least of My brothers, sin against the law of life and will suffer under this. Likewise, they will be tied to those whom they disdained. Therefore, be careful and pradtice self-control. It is not what goes into your mouth that debases your soul, but what goes out of your mouth burdens the soul and the person.

"Woe unto you when all people speak well of you, for so did their forefathers with the false prophets."

If you flatter your fellow people, so that they praise you and hold you in esteem, then you are like the counterfeiters who, for the sake of their own advantage, pay with false money.

It was and is similar with the false prophets, as well. They were and are esteemed by the people because they flattered the people and because those of high standing among the people were in league with them, having promised themselves personal profit and gain through this.

Recognize, you people in the Kingdom of Peace: In the sinful world, many righteous prophets and enlightened men and women were slandered and persecuted by the rich and powerful of this world, by church leaders and their adherents, and many of them were tortured and killed. At all times, the satanic used as tools those who wanted to keep and increase their earthly wealth for themselves, who strove for power and also those who were servile to the rich and powerful.

You should know this, so that you understand why the old sinful world perished in such a cruel way.

False prophets were, among other things, also those who may very well have preached the gospel of love, but did not live accordingly themselves. And they were also all those who called themselves "Christian" and behaved in an un-christian way in their life. They were often lauded for their eloquence and were honored and praised because of their wealth and prestige.

Oh see, nevertheless and in the course of time, all true prophets and enlightened ones contributed to the fact that the crystal of inner life, with its many facets of eternal truth, sparkled and shone ever more. In this way, the Kingdom of God on Earth very gradually built up.

It is important for you, dear brothers and sisters in the Kingdom of Peace, to nourish and cherish, tend and safeguard this now perfect, sparkling and shining crystal, the inner life, like a precious flower. It is the law of the Love and Wisdom of God, His Order, His Will, His Wisdom, His Earnestness, His Kindness, His infinite Love-radiation, and His Meekness.

You are the salt of the Earth

You are the salt of the Earth, for every sacrifice must be salted with salt, but if the salt has lost its taste, with what shall one salt? Henceforth, it is good for nothing, but to be poured out and trodden underfoot. (Chap. 25:6)

Christ explains, corrects
and deepens the word:

The righteous are the salt of the Earth.

They will repeatedly point out the deplorable state of affairs in this world and lay their finger on the wounds of sin. For much damage has been and is being done in this still sinful world—and many people became victims for the sake of the gospel.

The righteous who became victims shall be rehabilitated by righteous men and women, for everything shall become manifest through the salt of the Earth. Now, in this time of radical change from the old, sinful world to the New Era, the Era of Light, the righteous will bring injustice to light and will cause it to become evident, so that those who have done wrong may recognize themselves and atone for it.

However, you righteous ones who are the salt of the Earth beware that the salt does not lose its taste, that is, that you therefore remain in righteousness and do not let yourselves be led astray. For who shall bring righteousness into this world and who shall point out the deplorable state of affairs and sins that people have created? Surely, only those who know My name and are recorded in the book of the lamb.

The one who is no longer the salt of the Earth falls among those who have and are abusing My name for their own purposes and have persecuted, slandered and killed the righteous.

When the salt of the Earth loses its taste and the people disregard their neighbor, they will succumb to their own causes; figuratively speaking, they will trample themselves underfoot. Their unexpiated causes will then bring about illness, infirmity and grief. The light-poor soul will live in want and will feel on its own soul body what it has caused to its neighbor.

You are the light of the world

You are the light of the world. The city that is built on a hill cannot be concealed. Neither does one light a candle and put it under a bushel, but on a candlestick; and it gives light to all who are in the house. Let your light so shine before the people, that they may see your good works and praise your Father who is in heaven. (Chap. 25:7)

Christ, explains, corrects
and deepens the word:

I Am the light of the world.

In the mighty turn of time, ever more hearts were ignited by My light. The people recognized the eternal truth in My words. Ever more people walked the Inner Path and accepted the gift of life, the teachings and lessons from the eternal truth, in order to draw closer to God, the eternal Being.

Many men and women became My faithful ones, for they fulfilled the Will of God. They became brothers and sisters in My Spirit and became the pioneers for the New Era, who laid the foundation of the Kingdom of God on Earth and began to build upon it.

You should not think that I Am come to destroy the law or the prophets; I Am not come to destroy, but to fulfill. For verily, I say to you: Till heaven and Earth pass away, not the smallest letter nor one dot will pass away from the law or the prophets until all that is fulfilled. But behold, One greater than Moses is here, and this One will give you the higher law, even the perfect law, and you shall obey this law. (Chap. 25:8)

Christ, explains, corrects
and deepens the word:

As Jesus of Nazareth, I taught parts from the perfect law, from the Absolute Law, to the men and women who followed Me and all those who listened to Me. I also explained to them that the Absolute Law of love radiates into the law of sowing and reaping, since the Spirit is omnipresent and is also active in the law of sowing and reaping, the law of the Fall.

Through Me as Jesus of Nazareth, the incarnated Christ, and through all the true prophets of God that followed, the Eternal taught and admonished His children in the imperfect planes that the law of the Fall, the law of sowing and reaping, is constantly active. Those who do not stop and think it over and do not turn back in time will have to bear their causes as effects. The Eternal was and is striving, also in today's time [1989], to lead His human children and all souls to His heart, to the law of eternal love, before the harvest—the effects of the causes created by them—approaches them. The Eternal led and leads them to self-recognition through Me, Christ. He gave and gives them the strength to clear up what they recognized and recognize as a sin and shortcoming.

In Jesus of Nazareth, the Christ, who I Am, came to this Earth, into this world, to teach, as the Son of Man, the eternal law to the people and to live it as an example. This was done so that the people would recognize the path to the eternal Father and fulfill His law—and thus enter the eternal dwelling places again that He keeps ready for all His children.

The people who followed Me during My lifetime on Earth and who actualized the eternal laws, were My true followers.

In the following generations, there existed a Christianity and a sham Christianity: the true followers who freely followed Me, the Christ, by keeping the laws of the Sermon on the Mount, and the sham Christians who just talked about Me, the Christ, but acted against the laws. In addition, there was the so-called enforced following of Christ: This resulted from the forced Christianization of the masses carried out by the churches.

Recognize that there is no coercion in the eternal law. God, the Eternal, has given all His children free will. Those who freely decide have, with their free decision, the strength for what characterizes true Christianity: equality, freedom, unity, brotherliness and justice. All coercion originates from the law of sowing and reaping, also called the law of the Fall. It is given to humankind to freely choose its spiritual path. I, Christ, offered and offer the path to the heart of God, but I force no person to walk it. Those who force their neighbor live themselves under the coercion of the law of the Fall and personify the Fall-thought.

Several so-called Christian denominations force their faithful into baptism with water. Even the little children whose free will is not yet developed and therefore, cannot yet decide for themselves are forced, through baptism by water, into the membership of a church and thereby induced to participate in its other rituals.

This is an infringement of the individual's free will and, a forced Christianization, as it were. These are procedures in the Fall-law.

People who do not freely accept and receive Me, Christ, out of deepest inner conviction often have great difficulties to correctly understand and accept the Ten Commandments, the excerpts from the eternal laws. This is because these have been thrust into the background through many externalizations, dogmatic forms, rites, customs and cults. Within the denominations, these externalizations became the main thing, yet they have nothing in common with inner Christianity, the inner religion, but originated, in part, directly from the times of polytheism and idolatry, and thus from the spheres of the Fall-planes.

Only once people freely break away from the dogmas and rigid forms that have been forced upon them, from rites and cults, as well as from their own concepts of God, can they gradually be guided into their inner being, into their true being. There, in their inner being, they then find themselves as true beings in God and as inhabitants of the Kingdom of God, which is within, in every person. This inner life is the true religion, the inner religion.

Recognize that the eternal, all-embracing, universal law, the law of the heavens, is irrevocable. It is the law of all pure Being. The law of sowing and reaping emerged through the Fall and can be dissolved only through the actualization of the eternal laws. However, it cannot be evaded. The law of sowing and reaping will remain active in each soul until the sins have been recognized, cleared up, atoned for and surrendered to Me, the Christ of God. The Fall-law in the soul is then nullified. The soul is then freed from its impurity for the most part. It becomes again the pure being in God that lives the Absolute Law, since it strives again towards the absolute, all-ruling law of love and of life.

The law of sowing and reaping is valid until all that is unlawful is settled and transformed into positive energy, and every being lives again in God, out of which it came forth. To the same degree to which all beings from God have again been received into the heart of God, into the Absolute Law, will all purification planes—all part-material and material planes, including the Earth—transform into cosmic energy and again vibrate in the Absolute Law. The Fall-law is then abolished, and the love of God is conscious and all-prevailing in all Being, in every being.

Not one "dot" will be removed from the eternal law, which the true prophets brought before and after Me, and which I, as Jesus of Nazareth, lived as an example.

When it says, *"not the smallest letter,"* then it refers to a single aspect of the eternal truth, not the letter and the word of human beings as such. Human words are often merely symbols that conceal what is deep within. Only once humankind is able to feel into the language of symbols does it recognize the truth and the meaning of life, which lies deeply hidden in human words.

"The higher law" is the step into the perfect law. This will be taught to the mostly pure beings—that have come from the Earth and the soul realms—in the preparation planes, which are situated before the gate of heaven. The higher law is the last level of instruction before the gate of heaven. It shows the mostly pure beings how the lawful radiation is reactivated in the spirit body, so that it can be applied in infinity.

As Jesus of Nazareth, I taught parts of the perfect law, the Absolute Law. The whole truth still had to remain concealed from the people in those days, because they were still too attached to their belief in gods and oriented toward the various trends of belief of that time. For that reason, I spoke in the following sense: When the time has come, I, the Spirit of Truth, will lead you into all truth.

On the hill of Golgotha—this means, the place of the skulls—I was crucified by the Romans, because the Jewish people had not accepted and received Me as the Messiah. Although I preached, taught, healed and gave many signs of My divinity up and down the valley of the Jordan, the stubborn Jewish people remained submissive to the ministers of the temple, thus becoming partly responsible for the death of Jesus of Nazareth.

With the analogous words, *"It is finished,"* the Redeemer-spark entered all burdened and fallen souls. Thus, I became and I Am the Redeemer of all human beings and souls.

As the Christ of God, I acted and continue to act. In all generations up to the present time [1989], I gave and give My revelations through true instruments of God, through people whose souls are largely purified.

During this mighty turn of time, in which the Era of Light draws ever closer to humankind, I teach the eternal law in all its facets, and ever more people walk the path within, to the love of God.

Now the time is come, which I announced as Jesus of Nazareth, *"Today you are not yet able to bear it, that is, to grasp it; yet when the Spirit of Truth comes, He will guide you into all truth."* Now, in spirit, I Am among My own, the faithful wayfarers to the eternal Being, to the consciousness of My Father; and I teach them the absolute, eternal law, so that also those who will live in the Kingdom of Peace may fulfill it and thereby live in Me and I through them.

My words are life, they are the eternal law. They are preserved in the wayfarers to the eternal life and in many written records as well—as it is with this book—for the Kingdom of Peace of Jesus Christ.

Recognize that only the eternal law of love makes people free—not the law of sowing and reaping. This brings them only suffering, illness, hardship and infirmity.

Keep the commandments—only then teach

The one who breaks one of these commandments, which He gives, and teaches the people to do the same will be called the least in the Kingdom of Heaven. But the one who keeps them and teaches them, the same will be called great in the Kingdom of Heaven. (Chap. 25:9)

Christ explains, correct,
and deepen, the word:

The Ten Commandments that God gave to His human children through Moses are excerpts from the eternal law of life and of love. Those who violate these commandments, who merely teach them to their fellow people but do not keep them themselves, are false teachers. They sin against the Holy Spirit. This is the greatest sin. Such counterfeiters use the love of God, the law of life, for their own purpose. Thereby, they misuse the eternal law. Every misuse is robbery; and all robbers are a hunted and hounded people who, sooner or later, are caught and convicted by their own deeds, by their own causes. For God is a just God; everything will be revealed through Him, the good as well as the less good and the evil.

However, those who keep the law of love and of life, that is, who fulfill it in their daily life, and teach people what they themselves have actualized are true spiritual teachers. They offer the bread of the heavens to the people and will thus satisfy many. Those who give out of their own fulfillment are filled by divine wisdom and strength and, when the time has come, will shine like a star in heaven. For God-filled people draw from the stream of salvation and selflessly give to those who hunger and thirst for righteousness.

Recognize: Through such righteous men and women, the eternal law of love and of life comes into this world. Therefore, those who keep and teach the eternal law will be called great in the Kingdom of Heaven; this means that they will harvest a rich reward in heaven.

Live according to your insight

Verily, those who believe and obey will save their souls, and those who do not obey will lose them. For I say to you: If your righteousness is not greater than that of the scribes and Pharisees, you will not enter the Kingdom of Heaven. (Chap. 25:10)

Christ explains, corrects
and deepens the word:

The statement, "... *those who believe and obey will save their souls, and those who do not obey will lose them,*" means that those who believe and follow the laws of God will deliver their soul from the wheel of reincarnation, which will continue to draw them into the flesh until they have atoned for all that repeatedly drew them into incarnation.

Recognize that the mere belief in the law of life is not enough. Only the belief in the life and the actualization of the laws of life lead person and soul out of the wheel of reincarnation.

Those who do not keep the laws of God betray God and sell their soul to the darkness. Thereby, they cover the light of their soul, their true life. These people then live in sin and their soul lives in the slumber of this world. The law of incarnation, the wheel of reincarnation that draws the soul into incarnation, will still be in effect for some time, so that the incarnated soul may recognize that it is not of this world, but is in the earthly garment to discard what is human—and to uncover what is divine: its true eternal life.

Not all who know the written characters interpret them solely according to the letter—but according to the meaning. For this reason, it should say: If your righteousness is not greater than that of the many scribes—who pretend to be righteous and teach My law, but do not keep it themselves—you will not enter the Kingdom of Heaven.

Therefore, do not tie yourselves to the opinions and views of people. Actualize what you have recognized from the law of life; then you will recognize the further steps to the higher spiritual principles.

Recognize that the justice of God is the Love and Wisdom of God. Those who do not bring them to unfoldment in themselves do not radiate them; they neither perceive the depth of eternal Being nor fathom their true life. Their earthly life is a state of vegetation. Vegetating, they pass by the true life. On this side of life as well as in the beyond, they are the spiritually dead. Neither in this earthly existence nor in the life beyond do they have the right orientation, because they did not live according to the laws of life. They are not wise, but pass on only their stored knowledge. Thus, they become an adherent of sin and finally, a sinner. They act against the eternal law and through this, fall deeper and deeper into the law of sowing and reaping.

Reconcile with your neighbor

Therefore, when you offer your gift on the altar and remember that your brother has something against you, leave your gift before the altar, go there first and reconcile with your brother, and then come and offer your gift. (Chap. 25:11)

Christ explains, corrects
and deepens the word:

When you devote your life to Me, the Christ, and want to surrender your faults and sins to Me, and you recognize that you have not yet reconciled with your neighbor, then first leave your sin lying before the inner altar. Go to your neighbor and reconcile with your neighbor—and, if you no longer want to do the same or similar thing that led to the sin, then lay your sin upon the altar. The altar is in the innermost part of your temple of flesh and bone. The spirit of love and of life will then transform the sin into strength and life. You will attain liberation from what you freely, willingly and without coercion surrender to Me and thus, no longer do the same or similar thing. Your soul will then increasingly receive thc light from Me.

Take heed of the following lawful principle: When you have sinned against your neighbors exclusively in thoughts, through unloving, envious, vengeful, jealous or hate-filled thoughts, then do not go to them to talk about it. Know that your neighbors do not know your world of thoughts. If you let it become manifest in words, they will think about it. Come solely to Me, the Christ, who I Am in your inner being, and repent of your thoughts and, at the same time, send positive, selfless thoughts to the soul of your neighbors, thoughts of asking for forgiveness and thoughts of inner unity. Then I will undo what was caused in thoughts. And if you no longer think the same or similar thing, then it is already forgiven you.

Recognize that if you speak to your neighbors about your human thoughts, you might possibly stir up in them some human aspect that is just in the process of transformation. It could then break out once more in your neighbors, who will then begin to think and speak negatively again and burden themselves anew.

The law is: Through your wrong behavior not only those who are stimulated to think about it again burden themselves, but you, too, burden yourself, when you express your thoughts and, with this, activate in your neighbor the humanness that was in the process of transformation.

However, if unlawful things leave your mouth by accusing and insulting your neighbors and speaking ill of them—even if they hear it from a second or third party—then go to them and ask for forgiveness. If they have forgiven you, so has the eternal heavenly Father in Me, the Christ, also forgiven you. But if they have not forgiven you, then your heavenly Father in Me, the Christ, will not be able to forgive you either. Nevertheless, the love of the Father-Mother-God will touch the still rigid heart more and more, so that the person may think things over sooner and forgive you, and so that God in Me, the Christ, can also forgive you; then all that was once unlawful is annulled and transformed.

Beware of your own tongue! For the unlawful things that leave your mouth can do much greater harm to your neighbor and to yourself than your thoughts, which you have recognized and surrendered to Me, the Christ in you, in time—before they have taken effect.

Recognize a further spiritual principle: You cannot see nor hear thoughts—and yet they are there. They vibrate in the atmosphere and can influence the one who thinks the same or like things. If you surrender them to Me in time, they are nullified—unless the soul of your neighbor has already registered them in itself. Then you will be guided in such a way that you will be able to do good to the person about whom you thought negatively. And if you do good selflessly, without expressing your earlier thoughts, then what you unlawfully thought about your neighbors and that they already had absorbed into their soul will be erased there. And what your soul had radiated is erased in you as well.

Forgive—
and ask for forgiveness

Reach agreement with your adversary quickly, while you are still on your way with him, lest one day your adversary hand you over to the judge, and the judge hand you over to the guard, and you will not come out until you have paid the last penny. (Chap. 25:12)

Christ explains, corrects
and deepens the word:

Reach agreement with your adversary quickly, while you are still on your way with him, means: Do not let the sin that you committed against your neighbor remain standing. Clear it up as quickly as possible, for your neighbor is still with you on your path through life in the earthly existence. If their soul has left the Earth, you may have to wait until you can meet them again and can ask for forgiveness.

Recognize: The judge is the law of sowing and reaping. If it becomes effective, a person will not come out from under it until the "*last penny*" has been paid—that is, until everything has been atoned for that was caused and not repented of in time.

Therefore, use the chance to ask for forgiveness and to forgive as long as you are still on your way, walking over the Earth with your neighbor and the sin has not yet engraved itself into the soul and become a cause. Those who do not forgive or ask for forgiveness have to bear the effect until they have "paid the last penny."

Therefore, become one with your neighbor as quickly as possible. If the causes—for example, quarrel, resentment or envy—have already taken root in your soul, and if the same has also taken place in the neighbor, whom you are against, then it is possible that your neighbor will not forgive you so quickly—not even when you have recognized your sin and repented. The guilt complex may have hardened in the soul through the same or a similar way of thinking that you triggered in your neighbor. Through your sinful behavior that you nurtured over a longer period of time, your neighbor also nursed a grudge against you in the soul—and, like you, too, has thus created an extensive negative energy field, a guilt complex, that now has to be dealt with by both of you. Clearing this up can still take place during this earthly existence or even later in the realms of the souls or in further incarnations.

Recognize that before a blow of fate strikes someone, thea are admonished by the spirit of life, which is also the life of the soul, and also by their guardian spirit or by people. The admonishments from the spirit are the finest sensations that flow out of the soul or that the guardian spirit lets flow into the person's world of sensations or thoughts. They admonish a person to change their way of thinking or to clear up what they have caused. The eternal spirit of life and the guardian spirit may also stimulate people to go to those who are on the verge of being struck by a blow of fate. They will then approach the person concerned and will enter a conversation which will spontaneously refer to the matter in question. From this conversation, the cause of the looming fate may be recognized and cleared up.

Thus, you can see that the eternal light gives admonishments and indications in manifold ways and means—both to your neighbor with whom you have created causes, as well as to you, yourselves.

Through impulses by way of the day's events as well, people are admonished in time, before what was caused by them breaks in over them as fate.

Those who take such hints seriously and clear up what they recognized as a sin, by repenting, forgiving, asking for forgiveness and making amends, need not bear what was caused by them. If the sin is great, then it is possible that they have to bear a part of what wanted to break out of the soul, but not all of it. However, those who overlook and fail to heed all the admonishments, because they numb themselves with human things, will have to bear their self-created causes until *"the last penny is paid."*

Love your enemies

You have heard that it has been said: You shall love your neighbor and hate your enemy. But I say to you who listen: Love your enemies, do good to those to hate you. (Chap. 25:13)

Christ explains, corrects
and deepens the word:

The commandment of life reads, "*Love your enemies, do good to those who hate you.*"

Every person should see in all fellow people their neighbor, their brother and their sister. Even in apparent enemies, you should recognize your fellow people and strive to love them selflessly.

The apparent enemy can even be a good mirror for your self-recognition, when you become upset because of the hostility, which may have many faces; for when something on your neighbor upsets you, the same or similar thing exists in you as well.

However, if you are able to forgive your neighbor who has blamed and accused you without being unduly agitated, no correspondence is in you; that is, you do not have the same or similar thing in you and thus, no resonance for this in your soul. It is possible that in a former life, you already cleared up and atoned for what you were accused of—or even that you never built it up in your soul. Then it was only in the soul of the one who thought and spoke against you and accused you. Therefore, if no emotion reverberates in you, if no echo comes from your soul, then you were a mirror for this person. Whether people look into this mirror for their human ego or not—leave that to God and to them, His children.

Recognize that just the mere sight of you stirs their conscience and reflects to them that, for example, they once thought and spoke negatively about you. Now they have the chance to clear it up. If they do this, by repenting and henceforth no longer thinking or doing the same or similar thing, then it is rectified, that is, transformed, in their soul. Only then, will they see you with the eyes of the inner light.

A sign that the unlawful has been transformed into the positive in a soul is the good will and understanding towards one's neighbor.

Bless those who curse you

Bless those who curse you and pray for those who abuse you out of wickedness, so that you may be children of your Father who is in heaven and who lets the sun rise on the bad and the good and sends rain on the just and the unjust. (Chap. 25:14)

Christ explains, corrects
and deepens the word:

Those who keep these commandments are just toward their fellow people and, through their life in God, will guide many people to a life in God. God does not punish and chastise His children. This is already said by the words, "*... who lets the sun rise on the bad and the good and sends rain on the just and the unjust.*"

God is the giver of life, because He is the life Himself. From the eternal law of life, God gave human beings the free will to decide freely for or against Him. Whoever is for Him keeps the eternal laws of love and of life and will also receive the gifts of love and of life from the eternal law. Those who feel, think and act against the eternal law receive what they have sown, that is, what they felt, thought, spoke and did.

Therefore, everyone receives what they have sown themselves. Those who sow good seed, that is, who fulfill the laws of God, will also reap good fruits. Those who sows human seeds, which they bring into the field of their soul as human sensations, thoughts, words and deeds, will also harvest the corresponding fruits.

From this, you can see that God does not intervene in the will of human beings. He is the giver, helper, admonisher, leader and protector of those who endeavor to do His will, because they turn to Him. Those who turn away from Him, by creating their own human law, will also be controlled by their own human "egoity-law."

Thus, God does not interfere in the law of sowing and reaping. In manifold ways, God offers His help to His children; and those who sincerely pray to Him from their heart and fulfill what I, the Christ in God, My Father, have commanded them—to love one another selflessly—are in God, and God is active through them.

Accept your neighbor from your heart

For if you love those who love you, what reward will you have? For sinners also love those who love them. And if you do good to those who do good to you, what reward will you have? For even sinners do the same. And if you greet only your brethren, what more are you doing than the others? Do not even the tax collectors do so? (Chap. 25:15)

Christ explains, corrects
and deepens the word:

Therefore, accept and receive your neighbors in your heart, even if they do not love you, even when they do not stand by you and ignore you, by refusing to greet you. You, love them! You, stand by them selflessly and greet them—even if it is only in thought, when they do not wish to be greeted with words. Even a greeting from the heart, which is given in thought, enters the soul and brings good fruit at the right time.

Make sure that you act like the sun that gives—whether people want to see it or not, whether they wish for rain or storm, whether they want the cold or the warmth.

Give selfless love, as the sun gives to the Earth, and respect all people, all Being. Then you will receive your reward in heaven.

Do not flatter people. Do not discriminate, like people who associate only with those who think and act the same way and condemn those who think and act otherwise.

Do not bind yourself to people or things

And if you desire something as much as your life, but it leads you away from the truth, let go of it, for it is better to enter life possessing the truth than to lose it and be cast into outer darkness. (Chap. 25:16)

Christ explains, corrects
and deepens the word:

What the people crave for themselves personally concerns their person, their base ego. All this is binding. A binding means to be tied to people and things. Those who tie themselves to people and things, that is, who are tied to something, reduce the flow of cosmic energies.

If you bind a person to yourself only for your advantage, then, with your self-will, you pursue interests that lead you away from the life in Me, the Christ. You thereby abandon the impersonal, selfless life, entangle yourself in wanting to possess, to be and to have, and become impoverished of the spiritual life in your inner being. If you do not desist in time from wanting to possess, to be and to have, you will lose everything one day.

If you do not recognize yourself in the effects—for example, through the loss of all your worldly goods or in illness or in misery and in suffering—and then do not repent and make amends either, you will walk in the darkness as a soul and as a human being, because you were concerned solely with yourself, with your own personal well-being.

Therefore, recognize yourself each day anew and actualize the laws of God daily, and stop desiring something for your personal ego. Remain truthful—and thus, faithful to the law of God. Then you will enter the life that is your true being—and you will be rich in yourself, because you have opened heaven within you.

The truth that is impersonal cannot flow into the one who is not a vessel of the truth. Such people are concerned only with themselves and accumulate things only for themselves. This behavior leads to their turning away from God's eternally flowing power and to the life of a "stagnant pool": Only the unlawful flows into the pool and little flows out. This means that they will feel on their own bodies what they have accumulated in their stagnant pool.

On the other hand, the eternal truth streams into and through a person who is a vessel of the truth. They receive from God and give from God and thus become the wellspring of life for many. The cosmic energy of life, the source of all Being, streams through all forms of Being and through those human beings and souls who have turned to God, that is, who have become the vessel of God.

Recognize: The eternally flowing power streams only through the person and the soul that do not accumulate for selfish purposes, but give selflessly. Only through the one who gives selflessly does the stream of God flow unceasingly! If God can flow unhindered through a person, then this person lives in the truth, in

God, in the life that lasts eternally. Only such people give from Me, the life, because they are in Me, the life and the truth.

Become perfect as your Father in heaven

And if you desire something which causes another pain and sorrow, tear it out of your heart. Only in this way will you attain peace. For it is better to endure sorrow than to inflict it on those who are weaker than you.

Be therefore perfect, as your Father in heaven is perfect. (Chap. 25:17-18)

Christ explains, corrects
and deepens the word:

Everything that goes out from you and is not divine—like unlawful thoughts, words and deeds—can cause pain and sorrow not only to your neighbor, but also to you, yourself. For what a person sows, that person will reap.

The harvest corresponds to the seed. It is always harvested by those who have sown—not by their neighbor. Your neighbor did not sow your seed, and neither will your neighbor reap your harvest.

However, your seeds can have wings—like the seeds of different types of flowers, which, after blooming, are carried away by the wind and take root where they can hold fast. Your thoughts, words and deeds can also fall like winged seeds on the field of your neighbor's soul and sprout, if they find the same or similar conditions there.

The same or similar thing to what is in you is also in your niehgbor, if they become upset and angry by the words and deeds with which you caused them sorrow. Stimulated by your winged seeds, they think, speak and do the same or similar thing. You, however, have triggered it and can be called to account for it in the law of sowing and reaping. You are commanded to love your neighbors selflessly and to serve and help them—and not to cause them pain and sorrow by your behavior.

If your neighbors then burden themselves because of your unlawful behavior, because you invaded the field of their soul and brought causes into vibration, which they later have to bear and from which they have to suffer greatly, then you are tied to them. And if they, too, react unlawfully to your behavior, they are, in turn, tied to you. In this or another form of existence, you will have to clear this up together.

Recognize that a small insignificant winged seed of human ego can create a great cause, which already bears its effect in itself.

Therefore, recognize that every cause must be remedied!

Another example: If you send out your negative thoughts, words and deeds like winged seeds and your neighbors hear what you say about them, but take no notice of it, because they have no correspondence to it in the field of their soul, then only you will burden yourself; and you are tied to them—not they to you. Your neighbors can enter heaven because they have not accepted and received your negative seeds, since they did not think or speak in the same or similar way as you. However, if by your wrong behavior you have set causes in motion in your neighbors that would not have had to come into effect in them, because they would have been able to clear them up later without pain and sorrow, then you are the one who bears the greater guilt and have to bear that part you caused to your neighbors.

If, therefore, you have to endure pain and sorrow, do not blame your neighbor for your condition. You yourself are the instigator—and not your neighbor. Your pain and your sorrow are the seeds that sprouted in your soul —and also show themselves in or on your body as harvest.

Only I, Christ, your Redeemer, can free you from this—and only if you repent and no longer do the same or similar thing. Then the burden is taken from your soul and it will go better for you.

Recognize that those who realize that their pain and their sorrow are their own seed and accept their suffering show true inner greatness. This is a sign of spiritual growth; spiritual growth gradually leads to perfection.

The pure being is perfect; it is the image of the Father-Mother-God. It lives in God, and God lives through the pure being.

Blessed are those who are pure in heart; for they will behold God—because they have again become images of the heavenly Father. From a pure, devoted heart, flows meekness and humility.

Follow the path to within

Take heed that you do not give your alms before people, in order to be seen by them. Otherwise, you have no reward from your Father in heaven. When you give alms, you should not sound a trumpet before you, as the hypocrites do in the synagogues and in the streets, so that they may be praised by the people. Verily, I say to you, they already have their reward.

But when you give alms, do not let your left hand know what your right hand is doing, so that your alms remain secret; and the One who sees into the secret will publicly acknowledge it. (Chap. 26:1-2)

Christ explains, corrects
and deepens the word:

The Sermon on the Mount that is lived is the Inner Path to the heart of God. What people do not do selflessly they do for themselves. Selflessness is the love for God. Self-interest is human love. Those who do good for their neighbor only when the latter thanks them for it and praises their good deeds did not do it for their neighbor, but for themselves. The gratitude and the praise are then their reward. They are thus already rewarded and will receive no further reward from God. Only selflessness is rewarded by God. Selflessness grows and matures only in the person who has taken the first steps toward the kingdom of the inner being, that is, who has actualized.

The first steps toward this are to monitor and control one's thoughts: Replace egocentric, negative, brooding or passionate thoughts with positive, helpful, joyful, noble thoughts and with thoughts about the good in a person and in all that you encounter. Then you will gradually bring your senses under control. You will then no longer want anything from your neighbors either, and will no longer expect anything from them. In the further course of the Inner Path, you will speak only what is positive and essential. Thereby, you gain control over your human ego because you have learned to rest in yourself. Then your soul becomes more and more light-filled and, in everything that comes toward you, you find the good that you are then able to address and express in the right way. If you have learned this, then you will also address negative matters lawfully. In this way, uprightness and honesty awaken in you and you remain faithful to God in all things.

This spiritual evolutionary process toward selflessness is the Inner Path to the heart of God. Everything that you do out of selflessness brings you manifold fruits.

Therefore, if your sensations are without expectations and your thoughts are noble and good, then the power of God is in your words and in your deeds. This power is My energy of life. It goes into the soul of your neighbor and causes your neighbor to also become selfless. What goes out from your light-filled soul goes—sooner or later, depending on when the neighbor opens for it—also into the soul and disposition of your neighbor.

Those who give selflessly do not ask whether their neighbor knows what they have given. Selfless people give! They know that God, the eternal Father, sees into the heart of all His children and that the Eternal, whose Spirit dwells in every human being, rewards the selfless one when the time for this has come. This alone is significant.

Recognize that all good works, that is, selfless ones, will become manifest at the right time, so that those who should see them may recognize them, so as to also become selfless, in that they, too, accept and strive for the life in Me, and do what I have commanded them: to love one another selflessly, as I, the Christ, love them.

Learn right prayer

And when you pray, you should not be like the hypocrites who like to pray in the synagogues and on the corners of the streets, so that they may be seen by the people. Verily, I say to you, they already have their reward.

But when you pray, go into your chamber and when you have shut the door, pray to your heavenly Father who is hidden away; and the hidden One, who sees into that which is hidden, will publicly acknowledge it. (Chap. 26:3-4)

Christ explains, corrects
and deepens the word:

When you pray, withdraw into a quiet chamber and immerse in your inner being; for the Spirit of the Father, whose temple you are, dwells in you.

If you pray just to be seen or so that your neighbor may think you are pious and devout, then I say to you that this is not piety, but sanctimony; it is hypocrisy. Such externalized prayers are without power. Those who pray only with their lips or to be seen sin against the Holy Spirit, for they misuse holy words for their own self-interest.

Recognize that if you address God in prayer and do not fulfill in your life what you have prayed for, that is, if your prayers are merely a display of your ego and do not come from the depths of your soul and are not vivified by the love for God, then you sin against the Holy Spirit. This is the greatest sin.

When your prayers do not flow selflessly from your heart, it would be better not to pray and to first become aware of your thoughts and human wishes and to gradually surrender them to Me—so that the selfless love that is in you will grow and you will be able to pray from the heart. Then your prayers will be vivified more and more and imbued with the love for God and for your neighbor.

"... *And the hidden One, who sees into what is hidden, will publicly acknowledge it*" means that your thoughts of light and your power-filled prayers, which are vivified by the love for God, will one day bear fruit in this world. You are allowed to recognize your seed of love, and many will also recognize you as a source of love.

Find the truth in you

And when you pray together, do not use empty repetitions, as the heathens do; for they think that they will be heard when they make many words. Therefore, you should not do the same as they; for your Father in heaven knows what you need before you ask ... (Chap. 26:5)

Christ explains, corrects and deepens the word:

Only the person who has actualized little of the law of truth uses many words and empty, uninspired repetitions in prayer and in daily life.

Those who speak a lot about the law of truth and of life, thus using many words for it, cannot fill them with power and life, because they themselves are not filled with the law of God. Such words are egocentric and, for that reason, without love, even when they are chosen as if they were carried by love. Uninspired speech does not reach the innermost recesses of your neighbor's soul, and thus, finds no echo in those who let the love of God prevail in and through them. Those who speak without inspiration about the law of truth and of life, which, however, they do not actualize, merely stimulate a person, who hears this and likewise is still oriented to outer things, to engage in arguing.

Recognize that those who argue about spiritual laws do not know the laws of God. Everyone who wants to argue is convinced that they know better than their neighbor and want to confirm this to themselves. Those who argue only give evidence of themselves, namely, that they know nothing and are unsure. This is why they argue.

However, those who have found the truth do not argue about the truth, not even about what belief is. The word "belief" also implies not knowing: In the end, they believe what they do not know or cannot prove. Those who believe in the truth have not yet found the eternal truth.

They also do not yet move in the stream of the eternal truth. Therefore, belief is still blindness.

However, those who have found the eternal truth no longer have to believe in the truth—they know the truth, because they move in the stream of truth. These are the truly wise, who have raised the treasure, the truth, within themselves. The truly wise ones rest in themselves. This is inner certainty and stability. They do not argue about belief, because they have found the way from belief to wisdom, which is the truth.

Therefore, those who only believe in God without knowing the depth of the eternal truth, the eternal law, use many words about their belief.

Even in prayer, they will behave in a similar way: They use many words, since they do not inspire their words with selfless love. They are of the opinion that with many words, they are able to convince God or even persuade Him. They think they have to make themselves understood before God, because they assume that

God could understand their prayers in a different way than what they meant. Pagans think and pray in a similar way.

Recognize that the deeper people immerse themselves in the divine wisdom, the fewer words they also use in prayer. Their prayers are short yet powerful, because the word radiates the power that is lived.

Actualize your prayers

Therefore, when you are gathered together you should pray in this manner:
Our Father, who are in heaven, hallowed be Your name. Your kingdom come. Your will be done on Earth, as it is in heaven. Give us day by day our daily bread and the fruit of the living vine. And as You forgive us our sins, so may we also forgive the sins of others. Leave us not in temptation. Deliver us from evil. For Yours is the kingdom and the power and the glory in all eternity. Amen. (Chap. 26:5-6)

Christ explains, corrects
and deepens the word:

The community prayer, the Lord's Prayer, is prayed with different words and contents, because each community prays it according to the community's potential of love.

As Jesus of Nazareth, I taught the community prayer, the Lord's Prayer, in My mother tongue, that is, with other words, and thus, with another content as was prayed in later times and in other languages.

The words as such are unessential. What is important is that people actualize what they pray. Then every word that comes out of their mouth is vivified with love, power and wisdom.

You should not pray according to the letter or strive to pray word for word the Lord's Prayer, which I taught My own. What is essential is that you vivifiy the words of your prayers with the love for the Eternal and for your neighbor, and that the content of your prayers corresponds to your life.

People who are filled by the eternal truth, the love and wisdom of God, will, in turn, pray in another way than those who pray only because it was thus taught to them or because they belong to a denomination where the prayers are spoken according to the consciousness of the denomination.

People who are on the path to their divine origin pray freely, that is, with self-chosen words that are vivified with love and power.

People who live in My Spirit, who are imbued with the love and wisdom of God, who thus actualize the laws of God in their daily life will, above all, thank God for their life and for everything. They will praise and glorify Him and devote their life more and more to Him—in feelings, thoughts, words and deeds—because they have become the life of His life.

People in the spirit of the Lord live the prayer. This means that they fulfill the laws of the Eternal more and more, and have, themselves, become the prayer, which is an adoration of God.

Therefore, the one who fulfills the will of God lives in adoration of God more and more. Such people not only keep the laws of God, but they have mostly become the law of love and wisdom.

In the developing Kingdom of Peace of Jesus Christ, in which I Am the ruler and the life, the people will keep the law of God more and more.

Many of them will have become the law—and thus, God-people who personify the life, God, in all that they think, speak and do. Their prayers are the life in Me, the fulfillment of the eternal law. With their life, which is the law of God, they thank God for the life.

Therefore, gratefulness to God is the life in God. Their life, which is one single act of giving thanks, flows into the Kingdom of Peace.

They pray according to the following words which they fulfill in daily life:

Our Father, Your spirit is in us,
and we are in Your spirit.
Hallowed is Your eternal name in us
and through us.
You are the spirit of life,
You are our Primordial-Father.
We bear our eternal names from you.
You, eternal One, gave them to us
and placed in our names all the
fullness of infinity.

Our names, which You breathed into us,
are the Love and Wisdom—
the fullness out of You,
the law in us and through us.
Our eternal kingdom is the infinity—
the power and the glory, in and from You.
We are heirs to the eternal kingdom.
Therefore, we are the kingdom itself,
the eternal homeland.
It is in us and is active through us.
Your infinite, glorious will is in us
and is active through us.
The power of Your will is our strength of will.
It is active in us and through us,
for we are spirit of Your Spirit.
Heaven is not space and time—
heaven and Earth are one,
because we are united in You.
The love and power in us and through us
is our daily bread.
You, O eternal, glorious Father,
have brought forth in us everything
that vibrates in infinity.

Through us, You create
in heaven and on Earth.
We are in You, and You prevail
in us and through us.
We are filled in Your Spirit,
since we are spirit of Your Spirit.
We are rich in You,
since we live our heritage,
the infinity, out of You.
Our eternal heritage,
spirit of Your Spirit,
brings forth for us what we need
as human beings in the Kingdom of Peace.

We live in You and from You.
Life streams and gives itself.
We live in the fullness from God,
because we ourselves are the fullness.
The Earth is heaven
and the Kingdom of Peace
is the wealth of the Earth,
in which we live and are—
spirit of Your Spirit.

We live in the inner kingdom—
and yet are human beings who personify
externally what radiates in the inner being.

The name of the Lord is praised.
He is the life in and through us.
The name of God is the law of love
and of freedom that is lived.
Sin has been transformed—
the light has come.

We live from His light
and live in and from His Spirit,
since we are spirit of His Spirit.
In God everything has been cleared.
His name has made everything pure.
The glory of God be praised!
God's Will, Love and Wisdom
permeate the Earth and the land.
We ourselves are Earth and land—
Will, Love and Wisdom.
In us is the kindness of God—
the good from God.

We are in God and act out of God.
The Earth is the Lord's—
it is the kingdom of love.
It is active in us and through us.

The life, the glory of the Father,
is active in us and through us—
from eternity to eternity.

In its essence, this glorification is the life of those who live in the Kingdom of Peace of Jesus Christ. They live in Me, the Christ, and I live through them; and together, we live in the Father-Mother-God, and the Father lives through us from eternity to eternity.

Find the positive in the negative

For if you forgive men their trespasses, your heavenly Father will also forgive you. But if you do not forgive men their trespasses, your Father in heaven will not forgive you your trespasses.

And when you fast, do not look downcast like the hypocrites. For they disguise their faces, in order to appear as men who fast. Verily, I say to you, they already have their reward.

And I say to you, you will never find the Kingdom of Heaven unless you protect yourself from the world and its evil ways. And you will never see the Father in heaven, unless you keep the Sabbath and cease your haste to gather riches. But when you fast, anoint your head and wash your face, so that you do not display yourself before the people with your fasting. And the holy One, who sees into that which is hidden, will publicly acknowledge it. (Chap. 26:7-9)

Christ explains, corrects
and deepens the word:

The commandment to forgive and ask for forgiveness holds true until all that is not in accordance with the eternal laws is atoned for and cleared up. The commandment to forgive and to ask for forgiveness is a part of the law of sowing and reaping. It will be rescinded once all humanness has been cleared and every soul has become a pure, immaculate spirit being.

Thus, until then, the commandment holds true: Forgive and you will receive forgiveness. If you ask for forgiveness and your neighbor forgives you, then your Father in heaven has also forgiven you. But if you ask for forgiveness and your neighbor does not forgive you yet, because your neighbor is not yet ready to do so, then your eternal Father will not forgive you either. Those who have sinned against their neighbor must also receive forgiveness from their neighbor. Only then will God take away the sin.

The eternally just One loves all His children—including those who do not have the strength yet to forgive. If He were to forgive only the one who caused a sin to be committed and were not to forgive the one who was led by the former into sin and cannot yet forgive—where would the justice of God then be? Both of them can enter heaven only when their sins are cleared up.

For this reason, be careful of what goes out of your mouth and pay heed to your deeds, whether they are in accordance with the eternal law, that is, whether they are selfless! Something negative is said or done very quickly—but it can take a long time before it is forgiven.

If you have asked for forgiveness and your neighbor is not yet ready to forgive you, then the grace of God will become stronger in you; it will envelop you and carry you—however, He will not take away from you what has not been cleared up yet. God's mercy will then increase in your neighbors as well and, while taking into consideration their free will, will lead them in such a way that they may more promptly recognize their faults, repent and forgive you. Only once all those against whom you have sinned have forgiven you—that is, when everything has been cleared up—can you enter heaven, because God will then have transformed all the humanness into divine power.

God is omnipresent. Thus, He is also effective in the law of sowing and reaping. In everything negative is also the positive, God, the eternal law. Once people recognize and repent of their sins and faults, the positive powers will then become active in them and will strengthen those who have come to know their guilt to clear up their sins with the power of Christ.

Recognize the law of God; it is eternal life from eternity to eternity—everything in all things: Everything is contained in all things, the smallest in the large and the large in the smallest, the strength to forgive in the sin, and the ascent to the inner life, to the eternal Being, in the strength that is set free through forgiveness.

Therefore, the divine can also be effective in the negative, if a person asks for forgiveness from their heart, forgives and sins no more. However, the person must take the first step toward the inner life.

Recognize that everything you do—be it praying, fasting or giving alms—if you do not do it selflessly, but to be seen by your fellow people, then you have already received your reward from the people. God will not reward you then. And if you fast only because of your corpulence, you will not increase the spirit of your Father in you. However, those who take in nourishment in the name of the Most High and exercise moderation, fasting from time to time, in order to relax and purify their body so that the power of God can supply all cells and organs in the right way, are the ones who sincerely practice accepting and receiving in themselves the life from God, in order to live in this life. And at the same time, they will dedicate their life to God, the Eternal, in prayer, in order to gradually become the prayer that is lived.

Do not mourn your dead

You should do likewise when you mourn the dead and are sad, for your loss is their gain. Do not act like those who mourn before the people and make loud lamentation and rend their garments, so that others may see their sadness. For all souls are in the hands of God and all those who have done good will rest with their ancestors in the bosom of the Eternal.

Rather, pray for their rest and ascent, and consider that they are in the land of rest, which the Eternal has prepared for them, and will receive the just reward for their deeds, and do not murmur like hopeless people. (Chap. 26:10-11)

Christ explains, corrects
and deepens the word:

Those who mourn the dead are still far from eternal life, because they see death as the end of life. They have not yet reached the resurrection in Me, the Christ. They are counted among the spiritually dead.

Do not mourn your dead! For the one who mourns the loss of a person does not consider the gain of the soul, which—if it has lived in Me, the Christ—enters into higher consciousness spheres of life. For if its life in its earthly existence was in God, then it will also be in God in another form of existence.

Recognize that the temporal life, the life in the body, is not the life of the soul. The soul has taken on the flesh for just a short period of life, in order to clear up and settle in the temporal what it has inflicted upon itself in various earthly garments. The Earth should be seen as a mere transit station in which the souls in earthly garment can clear up in a short time what they cannot overcome so quickly beyond the veils of consciousness—also called the walls of fog.

When a soul leaves its earthly garment, a person cries only for the garment of the soul, and does not think of the soul that has slipped out of the garment.

After laying aside its earthly body, a light-filled soul will be led by light-filled beings, invisible to human beings, into that plane of consciousness that corresponds to the way of thinking and living of the person in whom this soul was incarnated.

Recognize that every soul that has left its body is still drawn for some time to those people with whom it lived together as a human being. Should it learn that its former earthly relatives mourn for its shell, this is very painful for the soul. The soul that is still close to Earth recognizes very well why its relatives grieve only over its human shell and why it is ignored as a soul by the mourners. A soul which has to recognize this then feels the first deep soul-pain after laying aside its physical body; for it learns why the person mourns instead of thinking of it with love and unity. Thereby, it perceives many a self-interested thought from its former earthly relatives. It cannot draw their attention to itself, because it is not perceived by them. What it says, they do not hear, and what it can see they do not see. But the soul perceives a lot.

I encourage you to think about this: Do you grieve when the snake sheds its skin, when it leaves its skin behind and slithers away?

It is similar with the soul. It leaves its perishable body, its shell, and goes on. Therefore, you are grieving the loss of the shell, and are not thinking of the soul! The person who thinks of the soul thanks God, who called the soul back to His bosom, provided the soul in the earthly garment made use of its life in God, and thereby drew closer to Him. Remember that for a light-filled soul, putting aside the body is a gain.

And if you mourn the loss of a person only before people, you are feigning to them. In reality, you think neither of the person nor of the soul. You think only of yourself. The soul that registers this recognizes that it has not been loved selflessly, that possibly it was there just for its neighbor's self-interest.

Many souls have to recognize that, while in the earthly garment, their earthly relatives and acquaintances lived through them. This means that, as human beings, they could not develop themselves and live according to their own characteristics, because they had to do the will of those who demanded of them what was advantageous to the former. Many of these souls perceive what they missed in their earthly existence and, for this reason, return again to the earthly existence. Through the veils of consciousness, they return to the Earth and again stay as souls among those who lived through them. Still others seek to live on Earth what they were unable to develop as human beings.

As long as people are tied to people or things—like possessions, wealth and power—their souls return to Earth and slip once more into new earthly garments. There are manifold causes and motives why souls reincarnate. If a soul recognizes, for example, that it is chained to its relatives through sin, then it often becomes resigned and gives in to the desire to take on a new body. Inspired by this desire, it lives on the plane of consciousness that corresponds to its spiritual condition and is taught there. Among other things, it is made aware of the pros and cons of a new incarnation. It then goes into incarnation when the stars, in which its pros and cons are stored—and thereby, its pathway to Earth as well—show the way to matter; and when an earthly body is procreated that corresponds to its spiritual state of consciousness. It then slips into this human shell at its birth.

The man who begot the body and the woman in whom the embryo grew attracted that soul with which they still have something to clear up together—or in order to walk the path of the Lord together, in selfless service to their neighbor.

People should not look only at their bodies, but above all, at the incarnated being in them, and should strive to do the will of God and not allow the human will of a second or third person to be imposed on them.

Recognize that even if you say, "I do the will of my neighbor, in order to keep outer peace," you prevent your soul and also your neighbor's soul from developing and unfolding as it is good for both. You prevent yourself and your neighbor from fulfilling the tasks which your souls brought along into the earthly existence: to purify themselves and to free themselves from the burden of sin, which perhaps was brought along into this incarnation from previous incarnations. Those who allow their fellow people to treat them like children—thus doing what others say although they recognize that this is not their way—are lived and live past their own actual existence on Earth. They do not use the days; they are used by those to whom they are servile and therefore, do not know their own path over this Earth as human beings.

Those who bind their fellow people by forcing their will upon them, are comparable to vampires who suck the energy from their fellow people. They do not know themselves and, at the same time, tie themselves to their victim—and vice versa, the victims who let themselves be drained also tie themselves to the former. Both will be brought together again in one of their lives, either in an earthly garment or as souls in the spheres beyond—and this, so often and for so long, until the one has forgiven the other.

If two people tie themselves to each other—no matter whether they did the binding or let themselves be bound—both of them have burdened themselves and both must clear this up together, so that love and unity can be re-established between them.

No one can say, "I did not know about the laws of life." I say to you that Moses brought you excerpts from the eternal laws, the Ten Commandments. And if you keep these, then you will not tie yourselves to each other, but will live in peace with one another.

Recognize that only love and unity among you show souls and human beings the pathways to a higher life.

God, the eternally kind One, offers His hand to each soul and to each person. Those who take it use their earthly life. They treasure the days and are also able to live them according to the commandments, by clearing up what the day shows them. As souls, they will one day walk and rest in God, with all those who likewise have used their earthly existence in that they have, day after day, recognized and overcome with Me, the Christ, what the day brought them and showed them—joy and suffering.

And if you do not mourn for your own sake the mortal shell that your neighbor laid aside, but rejoice in spirit that the soul in earthly garment has recognized its spiritual life and has prepared itself for it, then you will pray with gladness for your neighbor to the Father, through Me, the Christ. You will send forces of love to the soul that is now closer to God, so that it may go on to higher planes and unite with God more and more.

The soul feels the joy and suffering of its relatives. The souls that have passed away in Me, the Christ, feel linked through Me, Christ, with all those who still walk in the earthly garment. The joy of the soul for being remembered with love by its relatives fills it with strength.

Recognize that selfless, loving prayers give power and strength to the soul on its path toward the divine. It feels the unity in your selfless prayers and receives increased strength. Through this, it will more quickly lay aside the human aspects that still cling to it and thus become free for the One who is freedom and love—God, the life. The reward from God is great for every soul that earnestly strives to fulfill the will of God.

Recognize that only those are without hope who merely speak about their faith and do not live what they seem to believe in. In the last analysis, the doubters do not believe in what they pretend to believe. From this, hopelessness develops.

Where your treasure is, there is also your heart

You should also not gather for yourselves treasures on Earth, which the moths and rust consume and which thieves dig up and steal. But gather for yourselves treasures in heaven, where neither moths nor rust consume them and where thieves neither dig up nor steal. For where your treasure is, there is also your heart.

The eyes are the lamps of the body. Therefore, if you see clearly, your whole body will be full of light. But if your eyes are lacking or if they are dull, your whole body will be dark. Now if the light that is in you is dark, how great the darkness will be!

No one can serve two masters. Either he will hate the one and love the other, or he will be devoted to the one and despise the other. You cannot serve God and the mammon at the same time. (Chap. 26:12-14)

Christ explains, corrects
and deepens the word:

Only the person who does not believe in God, in His love, wisdom and kindness, collects treasures on Earth. Many people pretend to believe in God; however, you will recognize them by their works. Many people speak about the love and the works of God—you will recognize them by their deeds alone.

Many people speak about the inner kingdom and about the inner wealth, and yet gather for themselves personally in the barns and accumulate worldly riches for themselves personally, so as to be held in high esteem by the people.

Those who are concerned only about their personal well-being do not yet sense the bird of prey that has already raised its wings to destroy the nest and steal the wealth, which the rich person, the builder of the nest, calls their personal property.

However, those who strive first for the Kingdom of God gather inner values, inner treasures.

In the temporal, they will also receive all that they need and beyond.

Those who are rich in their inner being will not live in want externally. But those who are externally rich and hoard their wealth will live in want some day. Those who gather treasures on Earth, will find them taken away from them so that they may reflect upon the treasure of the inner being and be able to enter the life, the inner wealth.

The soul will lack divine light until it strives first for the Kingdom of God. And as long as it is still possible on Earth, a light-poor soul will again be born into a light-poor body and will possibly live in poverty among the poor. The recognition will come that the treasure, the wealth, is in God alone. The one whose heart is with God will be rich in inner values and will enter the Kingdom of Peace.

I, Christ, give you a criterion, so that you may recognize where you stand—either in the light or in the shadow, "For where your treasure is, there is also your heart," and there your soul will be one day.

Take heed! Those who read these words and stand at the turning-point of the old to the New Era should hasten, so that they can still find their spiritual life! For when the New Era, the Era of Christ, is manifest over the whole Earth and the inner life is lived, there will no longer be incarnations for those who strive for external values. Then, too, there will be no incarnations more for the worldly rich, so that they may atone, as the poorest among the poor, for what they neglected to do as the rich ones.

Once the Kingdom of Peace of Jesus Christ has taken further evolutionary steps, there will be neither poor nor rich. All people will then be rich in My Spirit, for they will have opened the inner kingdom. They will also live accordingly on the new Earth, under another heaven.

For this reason, be prepared to serve God and to serve your fellow people as well, out of love for God.

Recognize: No one can serve two masters, God and mammon. Only selfless love unites all people and nations. Both the human being on Earth and the soul in the spheres of purification will one day be led to the decision: to serve God or mammon, to be for God or against God. There is nothing in between: either for God, or for the satanic.

Strive first for the Kingdom of God

Therefore, I say to you: Do not be anxious for your life, what you will eat and drink; not even for your body, for what you will put on. Is not life more than food, and the body more than clothing? And what shall it profit a man, if he would gain the whole world but lose his life?

See the birds in the air: they neither sow nor reap, nor gather into barns, and yet your heavenly Father nourishes them. Are you not looked after much better than they? But who among you could add one cubit to his life span, if he wanted to? And why are you so concerned about your clothing? Consider the lilies of the field, how they grow; they neither toil nor spin. And yet, I say to you, even Solomon in all his splendor and glory was not arrayed like one of these.

But if God so clothes the grass of the field, which today is alive and tomorrow is burnt in the oven, why should He not much more clothe you, O you of little faith?

Therefore, you should not be anxious and ask: What will we eat? What will we drink? or: What will we wear? (As the Gentiles do.) For your heavenly Father knows that you need all that. But seek first the Kingdom of God and His righteousness, and all these things will be added to you. Therefore, do not be concerned about the evil of tomorrow. It is enough that each day has its own evil." (Chap. 26:15-18)

Christ explains, corrects
and deepens the word:

Those who worry about their personal life, about their well-being—for example, what they will eat and drink or what they will clothe themselves with tomorrow—are poor planners; for they thereby think only about themselves, about their own well-being and about their possessions. With this, at the same time, they also plan in their pain and woe.

On the other hand, those who fulfill the will of God are good planners. They will plan both their days and their future. However, they know that their planning is merely a guideline that rests in the hands of God.

They place their plan into the hands of God, work with the powers of God and let themselves be guided by God in the events of the day. For they know that God is the all-knowing Spirit and the wealth of their soul. Those who entrust themselves to God, who place their day's work in the light of God and who fulfill the law "pray and work" will receive their just reward. They will have everything that they need.

If God, the Eternal, adorns nature and clothes the lilies of the field, how much more will He feed and clothe His child who fulfills His will! Therefore, do not worry about tomorrow, but plan and commit your plan to the will of God—and God, who knows your plan, will fulfill for you what is good for you.

I give you an example: Good architects will carefully plan a house and pay attention to all the details. Once they have finished their plan, they will check it once more and will then submit it to the client who commissioned the building for examination. If the latter agrees to the plan, then the workmen will work according to the plan. The architect and the client will supervise the execution of the plan and will interfere only when something does not conform to the planning.

You should lead your life in a similar way. Plan each day and plan well! Allow yourselves time for some reflection, too, in which you can find inner stillness and think over your life and your planning again and again. God will also permeate with His will a carefully made plan of the day that was placed in His will. Those who carry out their plan in this way need not worry about tomorrow. Their belief in the guidance of God are the positive thoughts from which emerge positive words and law-abiding actions. Positive thoughts, words and actions are the best tools, because the will of God is active in them. This means that the will of God, His Spirit, is at work in every positive thought, in every selfless word, in every selfless gesture and deed. God will give good planners all that they need and beyond that.

Only those who do not entrust themselves to God, who let the days slip by and do not use them, worry about tomorrow. The people who take each day as it comes and then blame their neighbor when they fail in many things, when they are sick, when they go hungry, when they cannot acquire what they need for their daily life—are not good planners. They are anxious and egocentric people who attract what they do not want and what they fear. Those who do not plan the hours, days and months with God's help and do not place their plan and themselves in the will of God cannot be guided by God. Only those who entrust their daily work to God and conscientiously fulfill the commandment "pray and work" can be guided by God and are fulfilled by Him—they are filled with love, wisdom and power. This means that their vessel, their life, is filled with trust and faith in God.

People in the Spirit of God will not live in want. They are good planners, they are strong in faith and work with the powers of the Spirit. Only anxious people are concerned about themselves, about their small ego. They worry about tomorrow, because they are not centered in God and do not believe in God's wisdom and love. With this, they unconsciously open the barn for the thieves who come and steal. They will lose what they have taken and hoarded for themselves personally.

From the hands of God, human beings receive food, shelter and clothing. Those who place their life, their thinking and their work in the hands of God do not need to worry about tomorrow. They will have what they need today, tomorrow and in the future—and beyond that.

Therefore, those who live in the inner kingdom will not live in external want either. However, those who are poor in their inner being will live in external want. If today they live externally and increase worldly wealth for themselves and keep it for themselves personally, then they are poor in their inner being and will live in want, that is, they will be poor in another earthly garment.

Therefore, strive first for the Kingdom of God and His justice, then everything you need and beyond that, will be given to you by God. See the birds of the air. They do not sow or reap, nor gather into barns; and yet our heavenly Father feeds them. *"Consider the lilies of the field, how they grow; they neither toil nor spin."* Nature in all its diversity is clad more beautifully than the richest of the rich. Those who think only about their well-being and their full barns will earn their bread by the sweat of their brow, either in this earthly existence or in another incarnation—as long as this is still possible.

The right "pray and work" means to work for oneself and for the common good. Recognize that the lilies of the field—indeed, all of nature—are there for all people and give themselves to them in the most manifold ways. Those who are able to grasp and appreciate this will not have to earn their bread by the sweat of their brow. They will fulfill the law "pray and work"—for themselves and for their neighbor.

And when it is written, "*they neither toil nor spin*," this means that people should not think solely of themselves and work only to gain profit for themselves alone, in order to adorn and display themselves with it.

Recognize that all Being is in the care of God. Animals, trees, plants, grasses and stones are in the care of God. They are in the life of evolution that is guided by the eternal Creator-God. Since all life comes from God, the animals, trees, plants, grasses and stones also sense and feel. They experience within themselves the Creator's power of evolution that vivifies them and leads them to further unfoldment in the cycle of divine eons. The power of the Creator, the eternal Being, gives the nature kingdoms what they need. The gifts of life flow to the life-forms to the same extent as these are spiritually developed.

The eternal Father remembers every blade of grass. How much more does the Eternal remember His children who have already developed in themselves the evolutionary steps of the mineral, plant and animal kingdoms! The children of God bear in themselves the microcosm from the macrocosm and are thus in communication with all of infinity.

Yet how poor are those who worry about tomorrow! They show that they have not yet mastered yesterday, since they are unable to live in today, in the now, that is, in God.

The inner being of a person, the pure being, is the quintessence of infinity. Those who grasp this as a human being look within and unfold the laws of life, so that they may perceive everything external in the light of truth.

Recognize that infinity serves the person who thinks and lives in an all-encompassing way—that is, without limitation. People in the spirit of love are not self-centered, but all-conscious. They are in constant communication with the powers of God in all Being. Whatever they do, they do from within, with the power of love. They plan and work according to the commandment "pray and work" and do not waste the day. They know how precious is the day, the hours and the minutes and make use of the time.

Therefore, those who truly live do not worry about tomorrow; already today, they receive what they will have tomorrow. For those who live in God will not be in want, neither today nor tomorrow. Yet those who stay anxious and cling to their possessions will be poor tomorrow.

However, those who see themselves as cosmic beings, who fulfill the will of God without reservation, attain wisdom and strength. The lives of those who are filled with love and wisdom are permeated with the power of God. They will lack nothing. But people who worry about tomorrow and see the future as gloomy attract evil; they will have their burden each day.

Therefore, do not think anxiously about tomorrow! Plan with God's strength—and let the Eternal work through you. Then your thoughts are positive magnets that attract, in turn, what is positive and constructive. For thoughts, words and deeds are magnets. According to their kind, they attract, in turn, the same or something similar.

Do not judge your neighbor

Do not judge, so that you will not be judged. For you will be judged in the same way you judge others; and with whatever measure you measure, you will, in turn, be measured. And as you do to others, so will it be done to you. (Chap. 27:1)

Christ explains, corrects
and deepens the word:

You have read that thoughts, words and deeds are magnets. Those who judge and condemn their neighbor in thoughts and with words will experience the same or similar things on themselves.

Recognize that your negative thoughts, words and deeds are your own judges. "*With whatever measure you measure*"—whether in thoughts or in words and actions—so will you be measured yourself. Just as you disparage your neighbor, in order to exalt yourself, so will you be appraised:

You will know and suffer your own worth. And if you say, “What the one has is enough for them—the other one should receive more,” then one day you will have only as much or even less than the one to whom you have conceded less. Just as you treat your neighbor in thoughts, words and deeds, so will you fare yourself some day.

Begin with yourself

How is it that you see the splinter in your brother's eye and are not aware of the beam in your own eye? Or how can you say to your brother that you want to take the splinter out of his eye? And see, a beam is in your eye. You hypocrite, first take the beam out of your own eye; only then will you see clearly, in order to be able to take the splinter out of your brother's eye. (Chap. 27:2)

Christ explains, corrects
and deepens the word:

Only those people talk constantly about the splinter in their neighbor's eye who are not aware of the beam in their own eye. Only those busy themselves with wanting to extricate the splinter from the eye of their brother who do not know their own way of thinking and living. Those who do not know themselves nor their beam—the sins of their soul that are reflected in their own eyes—have no eye for the truth. Their eye is clouded by sin. They then see in their neighbor just what they themselves still are: a sinner. Only those who work on the beam in their own eye see increasingly more clearly. Then, they will be able to recognize the splinter in their brother's eye ever more clearly and will help to remove it, according to the law of love for neighbor.

Thus, those who speak negatively about their fellow people, who denigrate and slander them, do not know their own faults.

You shall recognize them by their fruits! All people show who they are, that is, their fruit. Those who get upset about their fellow people and make fun of them show who they truly are.

Those who first discard their own faults are also able to help their neighbor. This is why all who speak disparagingly about their brother's faults—and thereby does not notice the beam in their own eye—is a hypocrite.

Do not proselytize

You should not give what is holy to the dogs nor cast your pearls before the swine, lest they trample them with their feet, turn round and rend you. (Chap. 27:3)

Christ explains, corrects
and deepens the word:

It is not in accordance with the eternal law of free will that you go with the words of truth from place to place, from house to house, using your skills to persuade and convince, proselytizing to every one you get hold of.

That would mean that you do not hold the truth sacred, and do as it is figuratively written, *"You should not give what is holy to the dogs nor cast your pearls before the swine."* This means, you should not impose the word of God upon your neighbor. Those who think that their neighbor should believe and accept what they think they are convinced of still have doubt themselves and question their own belief.

To proselytize means to want to convince. Those who want to convince are not convinced in their own inner being of what they extol.

Therefore, be good examples in your belief and not those that proselytize. You can offer the content of your faith and leave everyone the option, to believe in it or not, to go along with you or not.

The freedom in God is an aspect of the eternal law. If your neighbors approach you of their own free will and ask you about your belief, they are taking the first step toward you; and those who are firm in their faith will then go toward their neighbors and answer them.

Those who are in divine communication with their neighbors will not tie them to their faith—but will communicate to them only as much as they have recognized and actualized. Only those people who have developed little selfless love will want to tie their neighbors to their belief.

Therefore, beware of the overly zealous, who want to convince you of their belief. Offer the eternal truth in the spoken and written word—and live accordingly yourselves; then, those who have recognized the life in themselves will approach you.

Go into your inner being

Ask, and it will be given to you; seek, and you will find. Knock, and it will be opened to you; for every one who asks will receive and the one who seeks will find, and to those who knock it will be opened. (Chap. 27:4)

Christ explains, corrects
and deepens the word:

Only the people who have not yet entered their inner being, the kingdom of love, ask, seek and knock at the gate to the inner life. The Kingdom of God is within, in the soul of every person.

The first step on the path to inner life, on the way to the gate of salvation, is to ask God for help and support. The next step is to search for the love and justice of God. The wayfarer finds the life, God's love and justice, in the commandments of life, which are signposts on the way within.

A further step is to knock at the inner door, in the little chamber of one's own heart. This doorway to the heart of God opens only to the one who has sincerely prayed, searched and knocked. The inner door does not open to the intellectual who seeks only external values and ideals. Those who doubt will not be received either.

Therefore, the one who asks, seeks and knocks must do so out of love for God and not in order to test the love of God.

Recognize that whoever just wants to test whether God's love really exists will be put to the test very quickly. The heart's doorway stands open to the one who lives in God. They need not ask anymore; they have already received, for God knows His children. Those who have entered the heart of God have already received in their soul. This means that the wealth from God shines more intensely in their soul and radiates through them, the person. The ones who have entered their inner being no longer need to seek—they are at home in the kingdom of the inner being. And those who have consciously taken up dwelling in Him no longer need to knock; they have already entered and live in God, and God lives through them.

Only those will ask, seek and knock who still stand on the outside and do not yet know that, deep within their soul, they bear what makes them truly rich: God's love and wisdom.

Give what you expect

Which man among you gives a stone when his child asks for bread, or a serpent when he asks for a fish? If you, who are evil, can nevertheless give good gifts to your children, how much more will your Father in heaven give good things to those who ask Him.

Whatever you want that people should do to you, do it likewise to them, and whatever you do not want them to do to you, do not do it to them either; for this is the law and the prophets. (Chap. 27:5-6)

Christ explains, corrects
and deepens the word:

Recognize that you should not demand from your fellow people what you are not willing to give yourself.

When you expect your neighbor to do something for you, ask yourself the question: Why do you not do it yourself? Those, for example, who expect money and property from their neighbor, so that in their laziness, they will not have to work themselves, or the people who expect faithfulness from their neighbor while they are not faithful themselves, or the people who want to be accepted and received by their neighbor, yet neither accept nor receive their fellow people—those people are selfish and poor in spirit.

Whatsoever you demand of your neighbor is what you do not have in your own heart.

It is unlawful—out of an attitude of expectation—to force your fellow people into acts, statements or ways of behaving, which, of themselves, they would not be willing to do.

If, in wanting something from your neighbor, you have recognized your expectant attitude, turn back quickly and do first what you demand of your neighbor.

All coercion is the application of pressure, which produces, in turn, coercion and counterpressure. Through such extortionate behavior toward your fellow people, you bind yourself to them and make both you and the one who was blackmailed into a slave of the baser nature. Coercive methods such as "I expect of you and you expect of me or each gives to the other what the other demands of the former" lead to binding.

What is bound has no place in heaven. Both, who are tied to one another, will meet again one day, either in the fine-material life or in further incarnations.

This form of binding does not apply to one's place of work. When, in your occupational life, you have freely taken a position in a certain field of work, and the responsible person gives you tasks that you should carry out within the framework of your job, you have already given your consent to that by joining the enterprise. You have freely taken your place in the field of work and on the work team, in order to do what is assigned to you. Therefore, when you choose a job, you should also carry out what is assigned to you according to the field of work you have chosen yourself. Thus, the statement, "*Whatever you want that people should do to you, do it likewise to them ...*" does not apply to a self-chosen occupation or field of work.

"*Whatever you do not want them [the people] to do to you, do not do it to them either*" means: If you do not want to be laughed at and ridiculed, or you do not want to be robbed or lied to, or you do not want to be deprived of your belongings, or you do not want to be treated like a child, or you do not want to be robbed of your free will, or you do not want to be beaten or insulted, then do not do this to your fellow people. For what you do to the least of your brothers, this you do to Me—and to yourself. What you do not want to be done to you, you should not do to any of your neighbors either—for everything that goes out from you, returns to you. Therefore, examine your thoughts and guard your tongue!

Resist temptation—decide for God

Enter by the strait gate. For narrow is the way and strait is the gate that leads to life, and few are those who find it. But wide is the gate and broad is the road that leads to ruin, and there are many who walk on it. (Chap. 27:7)

Christ explains, corrects
and deepens the word:

"*... Narrow is the way and strait is the gate that leads to life*" means that in every one who endeavors to walk the narrow path to life, the darkling makes himself known and shows them—as he showed Me, as Jesus of Nazareth—the treasures and comforts of this world. Each day anew, the satanic should be resisted and opposed. Whoever is not watchful will be servile to him.

Recognize that every one who takes the first steps toward the life, at first feels confined and restricted, until they have made a final decision.

For now, they should cease to do those things that they thought and did in human terms until now.

The first steps lead into the unknown—they are called belief and trust. Until the first steps are taken, the path to life is strait and narrow. The first hurdles that should be overcome on the path to the heart of God are called: Change your way of thinking and refrain from the old human habits! Repent, forgive, ask for forgiveness and sin no more! For every individual, this means a personal effort and an adjustment of everything that until now was customary to them.

However, those who persevere with My strength will leave the narrow path and reach the great road of light into the kingdom of the inner being, on which they will strive toward the door to Absoluteness, to the life in God, with those who journey into the light.

The person is tested each day: for or against God.

Those who decide against Me, by keeping all human comforts and everything that makes them human, will not be led into temptation on the wide dark road, since they have given themselves up to the tempter. Many indeed follow this road to ruin. They are not tested like those who walk the narrow path to life.

Those who have given themselves up to the tempter thereby also give their unrestricted assent to what they have to harvest on account of their seed.

You will know them by their fruits

Beware of false prophets, who come to you in sheep's clothing, but are inwardly ravenous wolves. You will know them by their fruits. Can one gather grapes from thorns or figs from thistles?

Likewise, every good tree bears good fruit, but a bad tree bears bad fruit. Every tree that does not bear good fruit is fit only to be cut down and thrown into the fire. This is why, you should distinguish the good from the bad by their fruits. (Chap. 27:8-9)

Christ explains, corrects and deepens the word:

At the end of the days of materialism, of the "time of avarice and greed," many false prophets will appear. They will talk much about the love of God—and yet their works are the works of human beings. Not the one who speaks of God's love is a true prophet and a spiritually wise person, but solely the one whose works are good.

The gift of discernment, however, is given only to those who first examine their own cast of mind: whether they truly believe in the gospel of selfless love themselves and fulfill what is meant by it, and, what they have already actualized in selfless love toward their neighbor.

You can recognize your fellow person and sense the difference between the good, the less good and the bad, only once you have attained some degrees of spiritual maturity.

Those who still condemn their neighbors and think and speak negatively about them cannot yet examine their fellow people. They lack the gift of discernment. They merely pass judgment and do not examine.

If you are still a bad fruit, yourself, how can you recognize the good fruit? The one who does not actualize the laws of God thus lacks the gift to discern between what is good, less good and bad.

Therefore, those who want to examine their neighbor should first examine themselves to see whether they possess the gift of discernment between the just and the unjust.

A good fruit can be discarded very quickly and the bad one approved, when the rotten fruit shows off with much talking and acts with a lot of seemingly convincing words and gestures.

Recognize that like attracts like. Those who are still rotten fruit themselves are closer to the rotten fruit than to the good fruit. But those who are selfless are good fruit and the good, the selfless, is also close to them.

Those who are selfless also have the gift to discern between the good, the less good and the bad fruit. Therefore, those who want to distinguish the good fruit from the bad fruit must first be good fruit themselves. Only the good fruit can recognize the bad. The bad fruit seeks like-minded bad fruits again and again, in order to go against the good ones. The bad fruits condemn, discard, judge and bind.

The good, ripe fruits are understanding, benevolent and tolerant, and are kind toward their neighbor. They may very well address the wrongs, but they keep their neighbor in their heart. This means that they no longer judge, condemn or convict.

I repeat: You shall recognize them by their fruits.

The good fruit knows the bad fruit, yet the bad fruit does not recognize the good fruit. The good fruit looks only upon the good, the bad fruit only upon the bad. The person thinks, speaks and acts accordingly.

Fulfill the will of God

Not all who say to Me: Lord! Lord! will enter the Kingdom of Heaven, but those who do the will of My Father who is in heaven. Many will say to Me on that day: Lord, Lord, have we not prophesied in Your name? Have we not cast out devils in Your name? Have we not done many wonderful works in Your name? Then I will declare to them: I have never known you; depart from Me, you evil-doers. (Chap. 27:10)

Christ explains, corrects
and deepens the word:

Those who merely call on My name and do not fulfill the will of My Father are poor in spirit, despite their seemingly spiritually effective speech and their seemingly courteous words, and will not enter the Kingdom of Heaven.

But those who accomplish selfless deeds without expecting reward or acknowledgment are the ones who do the will of My Father, for they act as they think and speak.

Selfless deeds result only from God-filled feelings and thoughts. If the thoughts are impure, then the words are empty and the deeds egocentric.

Recognize that those who appear to speak from the I Am, that is, who seem to speak My word and appear to accomplish deeds in My name, living well from this, have already received their reward. They will receive no further reward in heaven. Those who do selfless works of love and work for their earthly bread will receive the just reward in heaven.

Recognize that the spiritual bread is the spiritual nourishment for the soul. The bread for the body should be earned according to the law of "pray and work."

The spiritual bread comes from heaven and will be offered to those who keep the law of love and of life and also fulfill the commandment "pray and work."

God gives people the earthly food through the Earth. The fruits of the Earth require preparation through the work of the hands. Thus, the workers are worthy of their wage.

Recognize the difference between the bread for the soul and the bread for the earthly body! Both may flow from one source, yet the one is spiritual and is offered to the soul, and the other is condensed substance, matter, and is given to the physical body. What the great Spirit, God, gives to human beings for their physical body requires human work; for example, it must be sown, cultivated, harvested and processed. For this, a person should also be paid by people.

Only the one who does everything out of love for God and people will be received into the Kingdom of God.

Build on the rock—Christ

Therefore, I compare the one who hears these words of Mine and follows them with a wise man who built his house solidly upon a rock. And the rain fell and the floods came and the winds blew about this house. And it did not fall in, for it was founded on a rock.

And the one who hears these words of Mine and does not follow them should be compared with a foolish man who built his house on sand. And the rain fell and the floods came and the winds blew and beat against that house and it fell in, and great was its collapse. But a city which is built solidly, walled solidly in a circle or on the top of a hill and founded on a rock can never fall or be hidden.

And it happened that when Jesus had ended these sayings, the people were astonished at His teaching. For He addressed the head and the heart when He taught and did not speak like the scribes who taught only by the authority of their office. (Chap. 27:11-13)

Christus explains, corrects
and deepens the word:

Those who hear and follow My word develop their spiritual life. They found their life on Me, the rock. They will then stand firm against all storms and floods. After this earthly life, their soul will consciously enter the spiritual life and will be no stranger there, because while on Earth the human being already lived in the kingdom of the inner being.

The prophetic spirit is the fire in the prophet and in all enlightened ones. God did not and does not speak through them as those "who taught only by the authority of their office." The prophets and enlightened ones spoke and speak with the full authority of the Eternal, the speaking God, whether people want to accept it or not.

It is written, "He addressed the head and the heart." What the intellect, the head, absorbs is talked over and argued by the "head-thinkers." Despite this, many a tiny seed falls into their heart. Those who receive the word of life with their heart also move it in their heart, causing the good seed, the life, to sprout immediately.

But those who want to grasp the word of God with their intellect alone will have to later recognize—perhaps only after some blows of fate—what it is they rejected through their doubt and intellectual arrogance. They will have to recognize that the seed, the word of God that was given from the horn of plenty of life through prophets and enlightened ones, would have spared them much.

The way I thought, taught and lived as Jesus of Nazareth is the standard for the way of living and thinking of the people of the New Era in the Kingdom of Peace of Jesus Christ. In this way, I Am very close to them. They greet Me in the spirit as their Brother and will accept and receive Me as the Ruler of the Kingdom of God on Earth.

The Twelve Commandments of Jesus

The Twelve Commandments of Jesus

The Bible of so-called Christendom contains the Ten Commandments of God, which Moses brought to humankind, and also parts of the teachings of Jesus of Nazareth.

Through the prophetic word, Christ has now presented all the essential aspects of His life on Earth and His teachings, which go far beyond the content of the Bible.

The following Twelve Commandments were given to humankind by Jesus of Nazareth two thousand years ago. They are the commandments for the coming Kingdom of Peace on this Earth. They are a continuation of the Ten Commandments of Moses by Christ, the Son of God, the Redeemer of all human beings and souls.

And Jesus said to them, "Behold, I give you a new law which, however, is not new, but old. Just as Moses gave the Ten Commandments to the people of Israel, according to the flesh, so will I give you the twelve commandments for the kingdom of Israel, according to the Holy Spirit.

Who is this Israel of God? All those, from every nation and every tribe, who practice righteousness, love and mercy and follow My commandments are the true Israel of God."

And standing up, Jesus said:

"Hear, O Israel, Jehovah, your God, is the only One. I have many seers and prophets. All live and move and have their existence in Me.

You shall not take away the life of any creature for your pleasure or your profit, nor torment it.

You shall not steal the goods of another one, nor gather for yourselves more land and riches than you need.

You shall not eat the flesh, nor drink the blood of a slaughtered creature, nor anything else that harms your health or your consciousness.

You shall not make impure marriages, where there is no love and purity, nor corrupt yourself or any creature that has been created pure by the holy One.

You shall not bear false witness against your neighbor, nor willfully deceive someone with a lie in order to harm him.

You shall not do to anyone what you do not want to have done to you.

You shall worship the One, the Father in heaven, from whom all things come, and honor His holy name.

You shall honor your fathers and mothers, who care for you, as well as all righteous teachers.*

You shall love and protect the weak and oppressed ones and all creatures that suffer wrong.

You shall work all that is good and necessary with your hands. You shall eat the fruits of the earth, so that you live long in the land.

---

* Christ explained: here "honor" basically means "respect."

You shall cleanse yourselves every day, and on the seventh day, rest from your work, keeping holy the Sabbath and the feasts of your God.

You shall do to others what you want them to do to you."

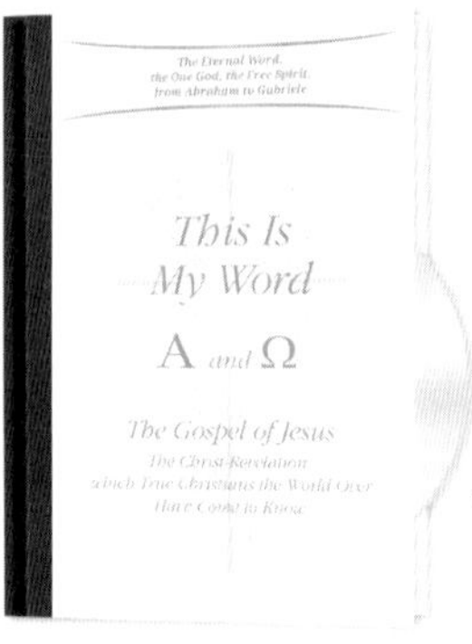

This Is My Word A and Ω

The Gospel of Jesus

The Christ-Revelation,
which True Christians the World Over
Have Come to Know

Jesus of Nazareth founded no religion. He installed no priests and taught no dogmas, rites or cults. 2000 years ago, He brought the truth from the Kingdom of God: the teachings of the love for God and neighbor toward people, nature and animals, the teaching of freedom, of peace and of unity. He spoke about the God of love, of the Free Spirit—God in us.

In the mighty work of revelation, "This Is My Word – Alpha and Omega," Christ speaks from the Kingdom of God through Gabriele, the prophetess and emissary of God, about the past, the present and the future.

In His work, which is a historic work, He directs Himself to all people, to explain what He as Jesus of Nazareth taught, how His life on Earth took its course, and He shows the correlations in the great work of Redemption that has its origin in the Kingdom of God.

An Audio-CD is included in the book with
The eternal word from the Kingdom of God:
"The Call of the Christ of God"* and *"The Appearance,"
Given through Gabriele, the prophetess of God in our time
1078 pp., HB, Order No. S 007en, ISBN 978-3-96446-313-5
Also available as an E-book

The Great Cosmic Teachings of JESUS of Nazareth

To His Apostles and Disciples Who Could Understand Them

with Explanations by Gabriele

Through Gabriele, the great teaching prophetess and emissary of the Kingdom of God in our time, Christ Himself reveals the laws of the true life, which He taught to the inner circle of His apostles and disciples 2000 years ago. For the first time in the history of humankind, His great cosmic teachings are available to all people.

The great cosmic teachings give us an understanding of the eternal divine law and allow us to sense into the life deep in our soul, which is our homeland, and we experience who we truly are—cosmic beings, children of the infinite love, on our way back into the eternal Kingdom of God, from which we all once left. The Great Cosmic Teachings of Jesus of Nazareth were interpreted by Gabriele and explained. She shows us how we can apply them in our daily life, in the family, at work and in our free time.

The Great Cosmic Teachings of Jesus of Nazareth are written down along with all the explanations given by Gabriele in a large, beautifully bound book.

880 pp., HB, Order No. S 181en, ISBN: 978-3-89201-951-0
Also available as an E-book